Beyond

The
Silver Linings

D. N. N. S. YADAV

PARTRIDGE

ISBN: Softcover   978-1-5437-0679-6
               eBook   978-1-5437-0678-9

Print information available on the last page.

To order additional copies of this book, contact
Partridge India
000 800 10062 62
orders.india@partridgepublishing.com

www.partridgepublishing.com/india

This book is dedicated in the loving memory
of my father S.D.S.Yadav

CONTENTS

1   About World Citizenship...1
2   Ecology Be Protected 5
3   Meet Your Life 10
4   The Learning Mind 14
5   The Company You Live 18
6   Beyond The Superstitions 23
7   Life Objectivity 28
8   Enjoy What You Do 32
9   At Peace with Nature 36
10 Life Action Plan 41
11 Never Fear Of Uncertainty.. 46
12 Universe of the Mind 51
13 Morality of Secularism 56
14 Attainment of Nirvana 61
15 The Clean Mind 66
16 Transform Energy - Can You? 71
17 To Be Self Aware 75
18 Understanding Relationships.....................................80
19 Broken Hearted At Peace..85
20 The Serene Moments..89
21 Care for Children 93
22 Law of Action..97
23 Zero-The Mind 102
24 Balancing Conflicts...107
25 Human Healthcare 112
26 Healing Force of Mind...118
27 Your Spiritual Strength..123

28 You - The Winner 128
29 You Think You Own..133
30 Fear Motivates You..138
31 Life Gives Options to Choose.................................143
32 You Have Life to Live...148
33 Giving Graciously 153
34 Recreate Yourself..158
35 Choosing the Right Path...163
36 Lack of Self-Confidence 167
37 Stress Makes You Strong 172
38 I Am No Body 177
39 Supreme Consciousness 181
40 The Light in You..185
41 You Feel Inspired..189
42 Judge Yourself Honestly 193
43 When Not to Speak 197
44 Mind Your Thoughts 201
45 Purity of Your Childhood 205
46 Flying with Thoughts..209
47 Living for Others..213
48 Reach Life Destinations 217
49 Your Graceful Mind 221
50 Not For Ignorance...225
51 Practicing In You..229

1

ABOUT WORLD CITIZENSHIP

What do we mean by citizenship? Being citizen of a nation? The moment we get citizenship of a particular nation not only we become entitled for certain citizenship rights in that nation but at the same time we become subject to certain obligations towards the nation and the fellow citizens. In addition to legal obligations there are moral obligations too. Honesty, integrity, dedication, industriousness towards the nation and amongst them the most significant obligation for any citizen has been the sense of belongingness for that nation. No doubt, the nation survives, people of the nation survive and also survives the civilization.

How about the world community? How about the world citizenship? Why to believe in old conventions which remained limited within individual state boundaries only? Can't national boundaries think beyond conventional limits? And break the outdated conventions in the greater interest of world communities. Above all is the larger interest of the peace, happiness and survival of the mankind on this earth. Do we believe in maintaining *status quo*? Are we *status quoits* only? There is no conventional reasoning behind perpetuating conflicts among nations of the world and no justification either. Establishing world community has always been a dream. Doubtless, efforts were made but they were not sincere and wise enough to inculcate a kind of feeling and confidence among the people who could be citizens of such world community.

Who doubts the honesty, integrity and dedication among world citizen? Do they have any scale to measure the 'sense of belongingness' among the world citizens? They do not have any such scale till date.

But for that 'international world politics' all is not going well. This would prove to be detrimental and damaging in all fairness for the global interest. World communities are made victims of international conflicts on various fronts. Those who are the worst sufferers of such conflicts are the poor innocent citizens of nations. They suffer for none of their fault. Since they happen to be poor small nations having no say of their own. That's it. The whimsical 'wisdom' of the so called world leaders in such conflicts has put the entire world community on the brink of nuclear catastrophe any moment. We fail to understand as to what stops these self proclaimed world leaders in making an initiative for a compromise formula where there is no clash of their 'self-ego'? We are able to establish a kind of sustainable world peace on this earth. Such 'clashes' if minutely examined are found to be more personal to these leaders rather than in larger global public interest. It should be kept in mind that any world community cannot be run by personal whims and fancies of a chosen few. That is the real source of trouble which hampers most of the peace initiatives all around the world today.

Alright, there may appear to be diversity in religious beliefs of different world communities. However, that's not so in reality. It must be noted that the diversities are merely in appearance only. The sole objective all such religious beliefs look for the mankind is the peace of mind for every individual irrespective of the fact to whichever community he belongs to. If one leads his life strictly in accordance with his religious considerations and follows the code of conduct provided therein then there is no reason to the world peace to be worried for. Our world needs to protect itself as an institution and provide such an environment which is purely secular and confer due respect to all the prevalent religious faiths across the earth. Giving due respect to all religions must be the sacred goal of our humanity. We need to give a serious thought to it at socio-political levels internationally, where lies the actual strength of world citizenship and off course, then the most desired world peace to follow. There are individuals who do not believe in any religion but this does not mean that they do not possess the feeling of respect for existing religions. Mutual sensibility and respect should be the rule for every individual world citizen irrespective of his caste, creed or the religion he believes in. You can see then the sense of belongingness and the feel of dedication among the world citizens for their world institutions. Come on...!!! The brothers and the sisters...!!! Let us move forward.

Looking to the present order of restlessness all across the world we should never ignore the humanitarian aspects of our civilizations. Let it be any nation on this earth. If that nation is suffering from acute poverty conditions, where people starve to death, small kids die of malnutrition then their very human existence on this earth is at stake. Is it not going to be a noble cause for the world citizens to be worried about with? Feel a humanitarian concern about it so that we can work upon it. May be it could be a fight of ego clash around. It could be with a motive to establish a kind of feel of supremacy over the other. Whether satisfying one's ego is in anyway going to best serve the mankind on this earth? If not, then how long this sense of 'being supreme' is going to 'prevail' that too at the cost of peace and brotherhood among the nations around.

What is wrong, if there is diversity on this earth among nations, and the human beings? Diversities could be in the form of language or their cultures. Diversities could be by virtue of the birth of an individual or due to religious beliefs. The territorial diversities of nations are but obvious. Are you going to consider 'sex' of an individual to be a diverse character on this earth? Are you in a position to say anything about the possibilities of life on this earth, minus the diverse opposite sex? No!!!...You cannot. Diversity is strictly a natural character on this earth. And how good it is if there is beautiful co-existence of such diversities on this earth? Diversities are beautiful. Yes!!!...Off course. Kindly notice varieties of flowers, plants, trees and other vegetations all across the earth. Seasonal variations are the beauty and strength of an environment. There are diverse categories of animals as per the requirements of existence of the mankind. So are the diversities in the nature of birth, religious faiths, language, territorial and the like. If the nature can balance variety of diverse characters so nicely, why can't we maintain a collective co-existence of such diversities on this earth, as human beings? This is for the sake of very survival of mankind and civilizations on this earth. Why we pass through kinds of intolerance all across the globe? All we believe that different religious faiths reach to the same destination. All political governments of nations also reach to the same destination that there must prevail law and order and maintenance of sustainable peace on this earth. Maintenance of peace cannot be exclusive it would be inclusive only. The feel of this inclusiveness would only be possible and would be able to establish sustainable peace on this earth when all the people are seen as world citizens. Why don't we go for a world citizenship? Every individual is born equal on this earth. It is for the political governments of the nations to confer and get enforced the natural right to equality to every individual. The feeling of hatred arising out of difference of region, language, religion, being rich or poor must be stopped sternly by means of making universal policies and ensuring its implementation in their true letters and spirit. The United Nations secretariat should come forward with a pious proposal to work on the lines for conferring world citizenship to each and every individual on this earth irrespective of his or her nationality. The governors under the umbrella of United Nations must ensure to its entire citizens the justice-social, economic and educational at least, if not political, by completely eradicating disparities among people of the different world communities.

"The whimsical 'wisdom' of the so called world leaders in such conflicts has put the entire world community on the brink of nuclear catastrophe any moment. We fail to understand as to what stops these self proclaimed world leaders in making an initiative for a compromise formula where there is no clash of 'self ego'? That we are able to establish a kind of sustainable peace on this earth."

2

ECOLOGY BE PROTECTED

Why there are all hue and cries around the world to protect the environment and maintain ecological balance? Ecological balance is very essential for survival of life on this earth. The very pertinent question comes to mind that are we destroying nature for the sake of grabbing power? Whether science and technology has given more strength to the desire of mankind to grab power? There is no doubt about it that people possess lust for power and this has caused lot of damage to this world. We used to learn in our childhood whether science is boon for the survival of mankind? If the science happens to be power then do we realize this fact that indiscriminate use of power would have its adverse impact over humanity and its sustainable existence? People have started misusing science to the detriment of human beings and the nature.

The basic motive of science now has become to be in competition with the nature. Really…!!!...Unbelievable. The point of worry is that as to why the science shows its envy to it? What the science intends to achieve by conquering over the nature, is not understandable? Mysteries of nature are the real power of the nature. Instead of unearthing the mysteries of nature the science should act in a manner to strengthen the nature by the power of science and this would be in further betterment of sustainable development of humanity with ecological balance intact. The science should not grow under this mistaken belief that one day it will be in a position to overpower the nature and replace it. This insane urge for power has completely destroyed the ecological fabric of the nature. The entire world community has on number of occasions expressed its serious concern over changing climatic conditions, indicators of the global warming and the global cooling, merciless destruction of forests and other natural resources, pollution of the atmosphere and its deadly impact over flora and fauna. People do not have fresh air to breath in and water to quench their thirst. The world has very often witnessed that the science fails absolutely when there is any natural calamity like Tsunami etc. When we start looking for the factors behind such natural calamities, it is found that the reason was manmade ecological imbalance making worst for the people to suffer whereas the science remains a moot spectator keeps waiting for the calamity to pass away and then only to take over the task of restoring the left over after thousands and thousands of people are dead and properties destroyed.

The scientific minds of our times have now realized the gravity of mistake which has already been done by the science in its quest to control the nature. Becoming powerful is understood but never at the cost of destroying the ecology of the nature. Intending to be powerful against the nature is dangerous tendency of the science and the people behind it. Why then the science intends to be powerful against the nature when it understands that it does not seem to be possible for it? In a most objective manner the science and nature can act in unison and prove to be complimentary to each other in the greater quest towards the existence of mankind, flora and fauna on this earth and keeping the nature's peace and its beauty intact. That's the real power.

We are seen expressing concerns at international levels towards deteriorating balance of nature. But in the name of doing, as if some favor to the nature, our activities remain limited only to the extent of calling for Rio de Janeiro, Geneva, New York or Paris conferences. Getting together, expressing concerns, doing nothing. No…!!!…That's not the way. Such worries we started only when it appeared if we are not doing anything now then it is going to be never. This nature getting imbalanced would engulf the entire mankind one day. We should remember that the nature never came out all of a sudden. It starts giving indications well in advance as warning signals that if we still do not bother to care, it would be too late. Such warning signals not only once or twice but on several times. The nature goes out of control when we cross all the limits and create a situation that water starts flowing above the head. We reach to a point of no return. This is deliberate and self suicidal. It is being said that the blind race of global development has started pushing the nature towards the brink of destruction. Now a clear line has been drawn to make it a battle between global development viruses existence of the nature. We need an extensive research on the points whether when and from where this race of 'blind development' started? And when, how and in what form it is going to stop? It will stop in fact or not? If it is not going to stop then ultimately where would we reach? Which are the nations in the race of development? Only few one's which have already become developed. A medium number which are still developing while a big number which are not yet developed and are still far behind in the run of development.

If global development has to do something with the nature imbalance then it needs to be identified as who are the real culprits for ecological disasters? Those who have squeezed the nature for their self gain became developed causing ultimately imbalance of the nature? There are the few handfuls of big nations which enjoyed the full pleasure of development. The other medium or small nations in fact remained deprived from such development. Nature then does not spare anybody. Uncontrolled development has released unlimited impurities in the environment. Development has afforded comfort to the people of big and rich nations. But at the cost of their comfort balance of the nature has been put to crisis by them. The poisonous industrial smoke has made the environment dangerous. While the share of development for medium and small nations is yet to take its shape, the nature has ringed the danger bell. The nations remaining undeveloped would finish undeveloped only. They would finish. Yes…!!!…You can't help but just shedding crocodile tears. Surprisingly the powerful culprits of ecological imbalance are seen organizing conferences around the globe. By expressing their bogus concerns they would make variety of regulations. International declarations would be made. Multilateral treaties would be signed expecting each other to enforce them. But in the blind rush for comfort development none would bother to enforce them. By the time the nature reaches further close to disaster. They would carelessly make no meaning of warning signals by the nature. Destruction and damage to the life and property of the people would be before us. The nations which claim them to be developed must not forget that they are still not developed in the sense that they would be able to stop any natural calamity from its devastating effect. Natural calamity would come down to earth. It could be in the form of disastrous cyclone followed by heavy rains or uncontrolled flood. It would cause havoc by burning out the earth or by freezing it ice below minus.

Climate change now is not a subject matter of forecast. It is now knocking at the door steps of world countries all around. We are realizing that we have exploited the nature to such an extent that any such knock is going to be disastrous only. We never know that our carelessness towards nature would give us enough time to be alert or not? The nature would leave behind its disastrous impact because our unlimited run for development has contributed only to breakdown the limits of nature. Then why to search for the blame elsewhere? We need to look within our own self. We would get a befitting reply. Still we can honestly repent for all that we have done to the nature. Arguments should be made on the points and restriction also need be imposed whether what should be the adequate limit of development for the nations? Whether other medium or small nations would get their share of opportunity to development as per their capacity or not? Knowing it fully well that the nature has been exploited and is being exploited, who would stop the nations liable of it? If they are not going to stop or no other nation is in a position to stop them then please...!!!.. There is no need to cheat people by organizing formal conferences? Making declarations which they know that they are not going to enforce anyway? Responsible nations should stop unbalancing the nature. They go on damaging the nature in the name of development. Entire ecological balancing of the nature has been hampered by them. The adverse impact of such imbalance is witnessed in the form of nature going absolutely unpredictable. Even the ultra sensitive machines fail to catch the devastating signals of nature and by the time people in and around the affected area are properly cautioned lots of destruction is done to the life and property of the masses. Responsible nations should strictly limit their development to the levels of justifiable necessity or else keep ready for deadly natural calamities. Innocents would keep dying. There would be none to cry for them. The burning question would be that as to why the innocent should for no fault of their own? Such kinds of man induced catastrophes need to be dealt with heavy hand by the world communities particularly those which are worst sufferers. A day would come when you are left with no option but to keep watching by your own eyes the humanity being put to all destruction by your own misdeeds. You would have no reason to repent with. Lack of will power on part of the world communities and their dishonest attitude is the major factor responsible. If timely action is not taken then it would possibly be the destiny of the mankind to get destroyed by its own hands. Do not blame anyone. Visualize a situation that no one would be left behind to blame or to be getting blamed. Keep ready for a crisis which you are volunteering. Today the world is witnessing worst ever human crisis since World War II in pandemic Covid-19 due to destruction of ecological balance. If still the world fails to take lessons then we are definitely heading towards large scale self destruction.

"Knowing it fully well that the nature has been exploited and is being exploited, who would stop the nations liable for it? If they are not going to stop or no other nation is in a position to stop them then please…!!!…There is no need to cheat the people of the world by organizing formal conferences? Making declarations which they know that they are not going to enforce anyway? Responsible nations should stop unbalancing the nature. They should strictly limit their development to the levels of their justifiable necessity or else keep ready for deadly natural calamities."

3

MEET YOUR LIFE

Never be upset in your life. Your life is full with experiences good and bad. Despite bad experiences life is still good. Like the darkness of every night follows the day and we hopefully look for the light of the day to come and mitigate the darkness. Always be hopeful in your life that its goodness would mitigate the badness around and you would meet your life. Look...!!!... This is an eternal truth that we just cannot escape to face with ups and downs in our life. We have to take the life as it is and enjoy it.

Have you ever noticed that we always live with fear of an unknown kind in our life? Fear about getting good job or losing a job. Fear about future of the kids. Fear about keeping good health or losing the health. Off course, fear about well being of your country at the hands of rusty dusty politicians. We are also exposed to the fear from the people who are dishonest and cheat us in our day to day life. What is the way out then? Life is like that only, nothing less than that and nothing more. What do you understand as to how to live in this world and lead our life? Means the way it is and the way we like it to be. There is a big difference in living our life idealistically or philosophically and living life actually or practically. Philosophical survival of life is impossible unless it is coupled with our actual day to day struggles. The real basis of life is a constant social and economic struggle, earning of livelihood and survival. We just cannot escape from our family accountabilities just in the name of being idealistic and philosophical. We have to struggle, earn and feed them and look for their better and safe future. If one in true sense intends to be idealistic and philosophical in his life, he can well attain this state of mind by means of putting through honest struggle effort after effort.

The question of the day would be that are you prepared to psychologically change yourself while living in this world? Changing or transforming in the sense that you would have to keep yourself ready for your day to day encounters with other people in this world. Such encounters may prove to be absolutely worthless for you. But you can't help. Even if you try to avoid they would make you to encounter with against your will. Definitely such useless encounters are going to spoil your life and would percolate down to peace of your family as well. There are categories of such people in this world who are like that only. They are not going to transform themselves. You need to transform yourself at least for your own sake while you come across with such people. That's the way you buy peace for yourself. That's the life in fact.

So…!!!… Did you meet your life? Your life is not yours the moment you are out to meet the world. Certain adjustments and accommodations you may need to make. Such adjustments may not strictly be as per your terms and conditions. You are going to feel hurt. Things are not happening the way you calculated them to be. You do all that at the cost of peace of your mind and certainly for the sake of your family. Such a compromise does never mean that you compromised with your principles. You are out to meet your life with all your principles intact. Welcome it for your own good, your beloved ones and fellow citizens. Never take it as your weakness or as a matter to be scared off. This would prove to be your real strength. Life is like that only. Enjoy the life.

The unknown kind of fear of your life has been such a fear which has not been generated by you. But it is induced by others intended to cause damage to you. You are well aware of your fear centers and you also know remedies about it. This way then you will not be able to meet your life? Make it a point that your fear centers are your own weaknesses. Who else than you can better understand your weaknesses? When you are able to know your weakness then who will remove them after all? If you are not doing anything then you will continue to be down under the fear. People would also not leave any chance to make you down with fear. You know that you cannot do anything by hiding yourself from the eyes of your life. May be you skip from the eyes of the people. Your life does not permit lot many things which are not in your interest. But still you do such things knowingly and continue to be down under fear. You fear not because the life will come to know about it but because others would know about it. You did not bother your life which is yours. You in fact bothered others who were never yours. I am of the opinion instead that your fear was never unknown to you. Some time you look back to your life you will find that your life always keeps preparing you to handle with such situations which made you fearsome. You will notice that you ignored all those indicators given by your life. So you were not able to achieve all that in your life which you have ability in yourself and you deserved. Why the kind of fear after all if you could not get a good job? Your life expected that you only would make an honest and laborious effort in that direction. You will reach exactly where there you will find that a good job is waiting for you. It could never be an unknown fear. How come could it be? We understand that still something was left behind to be done in your honest and sincere efforts for that matter. Here lies our mistake. Now we would have to satisfy ourselves by all that what we could get proportionate to our efforts.

Your good health is well in your own hands. Then there is no reason to scare with? The life has left everything on you only for you to keep healthy which means that you are situated within yourself. You just try to discover yourself. Are you able to feel that you are situated within you? If not, then ask to yourself as to where you are after all? Alright…!!!... Agreed... Your mind went around roaming without your permission. Who will stop it then? Your mind is not within your control? It is not situated within you. Then you are not keeping your health to be good. You became unhealthy. If this stage prolongs for a big duration introspect yourself. Where you find that you are not able to live within yourself then see to it as a warning signal that gradually you will continue to live unhealthy. You do not live in yourself mean you are living away from you. Oh..!!!...This is no way? Do not forget that by living away you started living away from your life as well. See...!!!... Then do not blame your life. Life is well around you. Since you do not keep situated within you so you are not healthy and away from your life. Remember, the fear of not keeping health has been created by you only and none else.

Take a determination in yourself to live with you. Make a habit to keep healthy you will see that you will never keep without health. You will meet your life then every day. When you will so keep your health intact then people with all ill will and dishonest intention would never be in a position to harm you in your life. Equally the fear of safety about your nation is quite reasonable in your mind. All those politicians who are not keeping within themselves would only cause harm to the national interest. But by the time a group of you all would be ready who are situating within themselves and would stop these politicians from doing so. When you are keeping health your ideological philosophy would become automatically stronger. It would be practical and quite close to the reality as well. Those self-centered politicians who are not situated within themselves means they are becoming weak and full of fear. You being with yourself mean being close to your life and free from any fear. Now you are able to meet your life. The beauty of your life lies in the fact that how you are able to make it more beautiful? You will appear to be great when you looked for opportunities to make other's life so beautiful. Then our life will not remain limited to few people only. Its shape would be much larger and exceptionally beautiful too. This only is the life in its comprehensiveness and in its meaning too.

"Oh...This is no way? Do not forget that by living away you started living away from your life as well. See...!!!...Then do not blame your life. Life is well around you. Since you do not keep situated within you so you are not healthy and away from your life. Remember, the fear of not keeping good health has been created by you only and none else."

4

THE LEARNING MIND

What do we understand by learning? What the role the mind has to play in the process of learning? Learning is a gradual and continuous process of mind. If a person has an alert mind and active one then his learning mind has no age bar. Those minds which are exceptionally fast learners have a sharp edge through regular mental exercise. Yes…!!!..It is possible. Learning induces movements within mind which is a rigorous process. But once this rigorous process has set in inside mental faculty it provides internal strength to it and learning process of mind relatively becomes much easier and stronger too. Retention capacity of your mind also becomes highly developed. Acquiring of knowledge by mind and subsequent retention of knowledge within mind both are equally significant. Have you ever studied yourself or have you ever studied your mind? Mind has a very natural tendency to forget about the things and retain only in the subconscious of the mind particularly which are so underlined. If the mind would not have the tendency to forget then it would have full capacity with information not so essential. This full capacity would disturb the balancing mechanism of mind. Forgetfulness of the mind creates space for newer information. Mind possesses a strange capacity to analyze and scrutinize information which is poured in from time to time. Nature of information the mind identifies to be preserved for future reference then it saves such information in the back of the mind. Such information remains intact for years and years altogether. As and when this information is required to be utilized by the mind in a life time then the mental processes download such information within fraction of seconds and put in application.

The aspects of negative learning by mind and also the aspects of positive learning by mind are the two crucial functions. If we carefully watch functioning of our mind then we notice that mind strangely looks more active and responsive towards negative learning rather than the positive ones. For e.g. if there appears to be any possibility that people are going to get easy money they make rush for it. There are only few who are not allured by such easy money. Putting hard work and then getting money is a rigorous process. Majority of minds who are even in influential positions prefer for easy money way outs by resorting to corrupt practice. Their mind actively responds to such possibilities knowing this fact fully well that it amounts to negative learning of mind. Positive learning of mind though passes through tough processes but gives the real spiritualistic strength and pleasure of the mind. The people with positive learning only have the real wisdom and are the only best rulers of the world on the earth. Let us always keep this fact in our mind that negative learning no doubt gives people an immediate pleasure but it is momentary only and vanishes like an air bubble. We need to go for an everlasting spiritualistic pleasure. How tough it may be to get it, this fact should not discourage us. Ultimate objective of man's life is the peace of mind.

Whether we would have to take our mind towards positivity or negativity this decision we have to take ourselves. Happening of all that would largely depend upon thinking of our mind and then on the fact whether with what objective we are moving in our life? There is no doubt that lot many objectives in our life are governed by then prevailing social circumstances too. Where our social situations are seen running towards a negative blind race and then without applying our mind we are also seen hopelessly joining the race. Do we ever think as to why our mind does so? Why we allow our mind to do that? It appears to be very strange whether mind does control us or that we control our mind? There are two big important factors in making of our mind and in directing its thinking process. If we talk about biology then in making of the mind many such characters are included through inheritance, which not only affect it constructively but they also influence functional nature of the mind. Bio-chemical studies of mind also substantiate these facts that various functional activities of mind are also induced by it and by the chemicals produced in human body. The chemistry of mind is not that complex that we need some specific process to understand it. But we need to understand the deep working mystery of mind whether our thoughts are influenced and controlled by the chemistry of our mind? Or else opposite to it whether our good or bad thoughts in fact influence the chemistry of mind? When did bad thoughts start creeping in our mind? Whether due to chemistry of the mind or due to our own reasons? Did the mind immediately receive any information? Or any such thought came into mind which was either positive or negative? Immediately certain chemicals started secreting in the mind which were damaging for the reasons that the thoughts were negative? Had there been good thoughts in the mental process then chemical secretions as a result would have been beneficial for the body and mind. The learning process would have been more strong and of permanent nature. Negativity would destroy the learning process of mind. Possibly you, within yourself, may not feel physically and psychologically better. This way you will fall sick then. This in fact is the reason behind that we often fall sick since we allow negative thoughts to creep in our mind. Not only they remain over there but they make their permanent stay therein. Ultimately our body becomes home for multiple diseases. We may go for medical treatments but it will not make any difference since we did not stop the negative thoughts from keep coming within our mind? We should keep ready for a downward oblique growth not only for ourselves but for our nearer and dearer too.

We should not forget at the same time that clusters of negative information which we kept collecting in past years are lying dumped in the sub-conscious of our mind. Even if we did practice in stopping information from entering into our mind then what about those information which are already there within it? Till such information remains there in mind they keep making mind blow. We need to pick them out of the mind. This would be a rigorous and continuous process. What a good thing it would be when right from the sub-conscious mind to conscious mind there is storage of positive information only? Very easily it could then be concluded that such minds would be strong minds. Learning and decision making capacity of such minds would be compact and scholarly. It must be clear that the chemistry of mind does not regulate good or bad thoughts of an individual. The chemical processes within mind start only when the kind of thoughts is given entry therein by the person himself. Now it would depend upon the nature of thoughts whether the mind is going to secrete chemicals which are harmful or beneficial to the body? A learning mind has to control its own thoughts.

Hereditary chemicals influence the thinking of mind. But researches would reveal the fact that despite hereditary negative chemicals if an environment of positive thinking has been created around the mind then its learning process would destroy the negative hereditary chemicals and the positivity would dominate. Therefore, the condition would be that positive learning of mind would be a sustained process depending in accordance with the environment it has been kept in. It is not necessary that children of a criminal would also have criminal tendency. Do not go to his negative hereditary chemicals. The existing social system should bother only to provide him a healthy positive environment. That's it..!!!... It would be our liability to provide a healthy environment and a positive direction to the learning process of our minds. Definitely then, this society would not fall sick and would become healthy, active and strong.

"It must be clear that the chemistry of mind does not regulate good or bad thoughts of an individual. The chemical processes within mind start only when the kind of thoughts is given entry therein by the person himself. Now it would depend upon the nature of thoughts whether the mind is going to secrete chemicals which are harmful or beneficial to the body? A learning mind has to control its own thoughts."

5

THE COMPANY YOU LIVE

There is maxim which is generally used for the purposes of interpretation of statutory provisions by the Courts. The maxim is 'nositure-a-soicis'. The literal meaning of this maxim is 'known by association'. There are words in the statutes which are used in association with certain words. Meaning of such words is made out of the meaning of the words in whose association such word is kept by the law makers. The meaning of a word is understood with reference to the company of the words it keeps. Same principle is applicable in case of our behaviors also. A person is known by the company he lives in. If we are living in the company of good people we would also earn a good name. Opposite to it, if we are in the company of bad people, it will give a bad impression about us.

Goodness or badness of a company relates with positive mindset and negative mindset. People with a positive mindset reflect positive energy in and around them. They think and do constructively for well being of the people and the mankind, whereas people with negative mindset release negative energy which is never constructive and harms to the people at large. Positive company has a motivational inspirational force. We start thinking and act in the same manner. One may cross question. If one wants to be a wealthy person then he should have the company of rich people. May be the rich people do not allow him their company. Good question. But never mind. Think rich. Make honest and sincere efforts and grow rich. It is the richness of your positive thoughts which would make you wealthy.

Develop a mechanism through your perceptive mind so that you can evaluate the company you keep. Spiritual growth is very important in our life. Do you wish to develop yourself spiritually? It will matter the company of the people we keep. Spiritualism should not be considered to be tough to practice with. It simply means ethical living and performing noble virtues in one's life. Learning by imitation is a human behavior. May be he imitates good things or bad ones, depends upon the nature of company he keeps. If we prefer to meet people with virtues frequently then one can observe we are bound to act the same way. Grow spiritually. It is the real sustainable strength in your life without which you will feel that your life, as if, never existed. You just lived and died. That's it. We need to understand the value of our lives and we never let it go waste. We would have to see the purpose of our life. We have taken birth on this earth with a fixed number of our breaths. The moment the breaths are numbered, our life stops then and there. Don't tell. Getting good company is not difficult. All the people are not bad. You have to see that the goal of your life is fulfilled. What would be the goal? That is to be decided by you alone and none else. Earning money could not be the only goal of your life. Your life's goal is even beyond that. Our company with likeminded people having similar goals would be able to accelerate the process towards life objectives.

There is no much difference between the people who are spiritual and the people who are spiritually realized. The people who have realized spiritualism are the best one's to breath into us the spiritual awareness. The spiritual values in our life are only possible by being in company of such people. The spiritual values so attained strengthen linkage directly with our heart and soul and make us live in peace and die in peace. Attainment of peace obviously has been the ultimate goal of our life. We should make others also to live in peace. Spiritualism has been an age old practice in Indian philosophy in search of peace and even all across the world. Saints would go to mountains to be close to the nature and realize the touch of spiritualism. Those who have realized the taste of spiritualism are nothing different than we the ordinary people. I am not talking in terms of any religious practice which could be any component to any person for spiritual attainment. All religions have their own virtues to practice with. This must definitely be for the betterment of the mankind on this earth. Even being completely secular one could be spiritually realized. Being ethical to the core of your heart and living with virtues in your life are the only essential elements for your company to live with and to attain the much needed spiritual strength.

Why do the people look for mountains in search of mental peace? In fact the company they get out there with the closeness of the nature matters. While you are all alone there but you are in conversation with the nature, the company you are keeping in. Imagine that moment whenever you went close to the nature. Remained there with nature and also conversed with it. Feel the closeness of the nature's beauty you would find out there. You find that you are lost somewhere not only for few moments but for hours altogether. Your mind went completely without thought of any kind. You feel that your experience as was never before. It would be an absolute zero state of your mind that too without any extra effort on your part. Yes...!!! It is possible. The company you live matters. This automatic attainment of your mind is spiritual realization in true sense. With increased intensity and the frequency you are living in company with nature, with increased durations you are there in closeness of the nature, it develops a kind of association and intimacy with it. This intimate relationship gives rise to infusion of the inherent values of nature with the individual's inner soul. The nature always teaches people that never to do wrong with anybody and always to give. The way the nature does without discrimination of any kind.

Without doubt where we live in worldly life, it would not be advisable to run away from our individual family liabilities and settle for mountains. Here comes the need for company of such people who are spiritually realized. We should not say that to be with the nature or to be in company with the nature is practically not possible in our day to day busy life. One can very well live in the company of the nature while away from mountains. The primary condition would be that he would need to practice and inculcate values of nature within himself.

That doing so is not at all difficult but it would be a continuous process to practice with. One can himself be spiritual by making himself aware to be ethical and virtuous. Once you are determined to be ethical and virtuous there is no second thought in your mind and you attain its zero state of your mind. Yes...!!! That is possible in worldly life even without going to mountains and still keeping oneself close to the nature. That's it. Now you need to give company to others and breathe into them the kind of spiritual awareness you have attained. It would not be enough that you become spiritually realized and leaving behind your fellow human beings. It would be against the nature and the ethical values. There are majority of people on this earth who are struggling for their mere existence on this earth. They may lack virtues sometimes just in their bid for survival. Do not blame them. Excuse them. Support them. Breathe in them your company.

It is noticed that there are people in our existing society who are quite innocent and ignorant due to lack of proper education. They are completely deprived of company with good people. It is sorry to say that people with good thinking and character do not like to allow them their company. Unless and until there is a universal kind of social acceptability for such endeavors it is going to be very difficult to inculcate in the kind of sense of brotherhood among the people in this world. Feel it once when you give your good company to those who are deprived of it due to various social constraints. This is nothing less than a big spiritual gain for you. You feel the kind of self-satisfaction you gain never before. Among all worldly relations you maintain, this company with innocent people would be of a unique kind of experience for you. Such people are so generous and kind that they only give you, they never take anything from you. Their company is so honest and pure that once you happen to get a taste of it, you would never afford to miss their company. Let us call it a behavioral company based completely upon human relationships which we need to maintain for the sake healthy and peaceful world community.

"Those who have realized the taste of spiritualism are nothing different than we the ordinary people. I am not talking in terms of

any religious practice which could be any component to any person for spiritual attainment. All religions have their own virtues to practice with. This must definitely be for the betterment of the mankind on this earth. Even being completely secular one could be spiritually realized."

———————————————

6

BEYOND THE SUPERSTITIONS

In an era of scientific advancement prevalence of superstitions is quite disturbing. Superstitions are based upon certain blind beliefs, irrational thoughts and erratic ideas which are linked with certain mythological stories and are given a kind of divine color. Sometimes it becomes very difficult to explain that despite scientific reasoning and rationalistic thinking superstitions survive. Are they so deep rooted into the social belief that people are not able to get rid of these superstitions? Man is not only a social animal but he bounds himself with certain religious beliefs which are prevalent in a given society and are followed by a particular group of society. Every religion must be based upon logic and rational knowledge. This proves to be a model code of conduct for the followers of that particular religion. It has been found that prevailing superstitious beliefs in a given society are mostly linked with religious considerations then it questions the very rationality of that particular religion?

If we deeply examine the nature of superstitions then it is found that superstitions make people weak from within. Under the influence and the fear of superstitious beliefs people lose their mental ability to properly think and take a reasonable decision. There may be a situation to be dealt with urgently but for the superstition people would either postpone the decision or would not take any decision for that matter.

It has been noticed that because of this state of indecision people suffer instantaneous losses also which has got no justification whatsoever. No justification could be given if considered logically but people with superstitious mind set come out with their own kind of unscientific reasoning which looks overshadowed with fear in blind faith. This means that there is no scope of any logical argument and discussion. It should be clearly noted that such societies are never going to be prosperous and progressive. Generations won't be able to take decisions boldly. They would always be apprehensive in their decision making as if something unknown would happen and would cause huge loss to the them either in person or property. It would thus be evident and is observed too that societies with logic and scientific temperament grow more rich, prosperous and happy. Since such societies have nothing to repent with for the reasons they know that they did not do any wrong deliberately.

Religious beliefs are considered to be psychological strength for the mankind. They not only provide moral strength but provide spiritual strength as well. Such strength confers sustainability to the human existence on this earth. But instead when religions make fearful and apprehensive of the superstitions then this is not fair and proper for healthy development of human mind. As once superstitious beliefs creep in, the human mind stops thinking rationally and starts working in accordance with the religious considerations behind a superstitious belief. He gets scared off the consequences under the impression that if he dares to think beyond the superstitions, decides not to follow them then he would suffer some loss or injury in the form of loss of life of some nearer or dearer or loss of property. These superstitious consequences make people weak and weak psychologically. Religious beliefs should not be weakness of people but it should be their strength. In a more rational and dynamic society of modern times we need to think beyond superstitions. Civilizations are progressive when they think logically. We need to come out of the bondage of superstitions and think beyond them in our ultimate pursuit to good for the mankind and for the progress of our society. This becomes all more significant when we know that we are living in an era of science and advance technologies where things does not happen per chance but are completely based upon existing facts and extensive research.

How to get rid of the superstitions should be the agenda of human life? We need to look for the ways and means to prevent superstitious beliefs from entering into our mind. I do not wish to describe any superstitious practice which is found to be there in our society. My only intention is to provide logical explanations to discourage superstitious practices making room in human mind. How could this be possible is the prime issue? Please do not correlate superstitions with any religion. No religions on this earth existing today go for promoting superstitions. They seek to promote human life on humanitarian beliefs completely based upon logical explanations. The logic has no room for superstitions. Superstitions literally are the fear consciousness of our mind. First of all we need to recognize and identify the agents of superstition found spread around in the society. We also need to understand as to what is their motive behind such practices? The only motive appears to be that they intend to rule the human minds by putting them under fear. It is the weakness of the people which they exploit to their own advantage. In recent times the agents of superstition have acquired huge monetary gains by practicing illogical explanations to the innocent people. The innocence of people could be attributed to their lack of proper education in any particular society. Even educated people are also seen having deep faith in superstitions. May be it could be a difficult task to persuade innocent people in the sense they go completely blind to follow a superstition. There could be no scope for any logical argumentation whatsoever. The situation becomes even more tedious to convince and argue with the people who are educated and still believe in superstitions. They have developed their own kinds of arguments to justify their acts and blind faiths. They do not appear to be ready to listen to any logic against since in their opinion it amounts to be interfering with their right to personal beliefs. It is agreed. That is true also. One may put forward an argument that he does what he feels to be right and proper.

But my humble submission is that one's belief about existence of any superstitious practice could be correct according to his individual considerations. At the same time one should not forget about the fact that such belief has not been based upon his own ideas and experiences. One practices such belief since it owes its origin from past. If I happen to develop a thought that by practicing any particular belief I would definitely be a successful man on this earth then possibly I am wrong. There is no miracle behind a successful man. It is only due to his sustained, hard and honest efforts he is putting in that he becomes successful. Do not look for miracles to happen. Do not allow the superstitious beliefs to creep in your mind. It is only your deeds which are rightfully going to decide your destiny. Make it a point that in present your deeds are not going to be controlled by any superstition. No way to keep waiting for favorable results without doing proper karma. Superstitions are not going to help you out. Always believe in your own self. That is the real force within you in the form of your inner conscience. It always goes for logics and never believes in miracles. Feel the force within you and perform your deeds honestly. It is quite convincing you experience yourself by sitting with your fingers crossed and doing nothing. No amount of luck or blind faith is going to help you out to achieve what you wish to be. No religious performance organized by you would work out to get desired results for you. Any blind faith to perform any ritual to get the situation favorable to you would be all wastage of your time, energy and hard earned money. In return you are going to get nothing. What you are going to get is loss of confidence, hopelessness and depression all around you. It's your well planned hard work only which is going to yield results in its entirety. Be assured that your life journey will reach to a logical end. Your own logics which are definitely not borrowed or dependent upon superstitions would finally work out for you a definite reach within your life.

"Religious beliefs are considered to be psychological strength for the mankind. They not only provide moral strength but provide spiritual strength as well. Such strength confers sustainability to

the human existence on this earth. But instead when religions make fearful and apprehensive of the superstitions then this is not fair and proper for healthy development of the human mind. As once superstitious beliefs creep in, the human mind stops thinking rationally and starts working in accordance with the religious considerations behind a superstitious belief."

7

LIFE OBJECTIVITY

Understanding the objectivity in your life is very significant for the reasons to understand the secrets of enjoying life. The secret of content life is that 'you are yourself'. None else but you are the only person in this universe who knows things best about you. Understand who you are? You have come in this world with a purpose. Everybody wants to achieve the life objectives. No one would like disappointment. But it so happens in life game that at one point of time you emerge to be a winner, whereas on an another you happen to be looser, may be for the reasons that things were not within your control. It must be remembered that not always the situations are going to be in your favor. Make your adverse situations favorable by means of your working performances. For maintaining the life objectivity you need to learn to balance your emotions between the two situations when you win or when you lose. Make sure life is like this only, a balancing combination of ups and downs which you have to pass through.

Never forget that you are living in a world which is quite unpredictable. It may put you on occasions in a frustrated state of mind that despite your sincere efforts you lost. But the attitude which is going to be a boon for you is your habits of self-reliance come what may. You are so determined of yourselves and your capacity to work that this unpredictable world has to give way to you to move on with your life objectivity. You will be able to win over this unpredictable world since you are confident within you.

Now the pertinent question would be that what should be your life objectivity? And once you are able to identify these objectives you will get the real taste of your life enjoyment. Your spiritual development should be like that you are less dependent on this world and you are more dependent upon yourself. Such independence would be sufficient enough to change our mind set with an attitude. We would start with a kind of feel to 'give' more rather to 'take' one. That is objectivity to dedicate your life in serving others and adding a kind of value and dignity to their life. There are people on this earth who are in need of your sincere help. More you give more you get for the pious objectivity of your helping attitude to needy persons. While you are offering your talent for the cause of others you will experience the miracle of spiritual development in your life one day. Offering oneself for the cause of others is no doubt a tough challenge. Grab this opportunity to grow with moral strength and spiritualism. This is the virtual strength within you that 'you are yourself' in true sense. If you happen to go through the life stories of great people in this world you will find that they were able to develop the ability to understand that what they are? They could identify their life objectivities. The ability to understanding oneself is miraculous experience. In real sense the feel of true life objectivity. This will make you with constant peace of mind so as to strengthen you to keep working for the sake of others who are the needy.

Do you consider that whatever you wished to achieve in your life, you have achieved all that? You think that your life objectivity is fulfilled then? But still there is no mark of happiness on your face. Why...!!! Why that victorious smile is not visible on your face? Why you are seen lost somewhere? That's the point. Meaning thereby that merely getting everything in one's life is not going to be sufficient. In fact the life is something else rather than getting all that. Have you not heard stories about such great people who relinquished their entire earned property just for the sake of getting life? Then they could enter into their life. What does it mean? That despite earning all property couldn't they get the life into it? The question now is that what in fact this life is? That even the entire property could not buy it? This appears to be a very complicated question. Probably looking to exact answer of this question would be equally complicated. We need to think upon it whether how comes this complication? In fact complications are in our mind. Complexities were bound to creep in specifically when we let them to come in. And once the complexities have made their entry in then they will show their influence.

We need always to remember that there are no such complexities which relate to an individual's life or having concern with his life objectivity. Virtually our thinking patterns make them complex. Then why don't we change our thinking patterns? Can a person change his thinking in this manner all of a sudden? Change in thinking means positivity of life not only being positive towards own life but having positive approach for them too with whom we live in social associations. Why this need to change of thinking arrived at after all? Is it because that we remained negative towards life? Whether this negativity is the sole factor behind our life complexities? It means we ourselves are accountable to make our life complex. Why then keep moving searching for the answers elsewhere? Why don't we look into our own inner conscience? This only is the weakness of a man. He himself creates troubles and looks for elsewhere. You would have to face consequences for the problems you generate yourself. No escape.

Try to remember those occasions you attempted to create problems for others? You thought negative for them and also that they should suffer loss. Albeit their loss was no way connected with your profit whatsoever. The only negative state of mind that individual suffers harm then you will feel good. If you have linked your benefit with the loss of that individual then this is also not fair. How good it would have been if you were in a healthy competition with that individual? You would have improved your ability on merits and have moved much forward by leaving him far behind. Then it would have become your habit to keep moving on and progressing. Nobody would have been there in competition with you. Sky would have been the limit for you. People who are great do like this only. They have no competition with any other individual. They consider it to be a negative thought. They compete with themselves only keep moving forward and become great. How positive is this life objectivity? We need to practice with.

When we think to cause harm to others we go negative. Now here it starts the complexity of our mind. We wasted our energy in pursing negative thoughts. We started feeling pleasure when others were in trouble. When they were happy then we became disturbed. Now no much energy was left behind so as to counter our disturbances. Oh…!!! What all that happened? It was not objective of your life. But who was responsible for that entire situation? You…!!!….And none else? Now you reached to a point of no return. You would not be able to either. You never thought of helping others. But at least you could have helped out yourself. What can you do now? Now death only is standing before you. Death comes to everybody. But it was not that fearful the way you are facing one. Now it is understandable that as to why there is no meaning of earned property? They lived their life in the search of life to achieve their life objectivity which they could achieve. They were least bothered about the complexities of life for the reasons that they developed positive set of their thinking patterns and did not complicate situations. It is completely for you to think fairly and work upon it. Yes…!!! You can do it once you are determined to learn and achieve your life objectives. Complications in life are nothing but our negative thoughts only. Help you out. Please…!!!

"We need always to remember that there are no such complexities which relate to an individual's life or having concern with his life objectivity. Virtually our thinking patterns make them complex. Then why don't we change our thinking patterns? Can a person change his thinking in this manner all of a sudden? Change in thinking means positivity of life. Not only being positive towards own life but having approach for them too, with whom we live in social associations".

8

ENJOY WHAT YOU DO

The foremost question of your life could be, do you enjoy what you do? Feel of enjoyment is the virtual perception of one's own self. You enjoy being rich, it's your perception. You wish to earn name and fame, it's your perception. May be you are not rich but still you enjoy your life. There are people in our world with abundance of money but they are not able to enjoy their life. They are not happy in their life. It completely depends upon you only as to what you wish to do? Or the way you wish to enjoy your life by your doings. Being ambitious is not bad but if you happen to turn overambitious this is not good because high ambitions are going to distract you from living in present. They would force you to think for the future. You will not be able to live in present. There would be strong possibilities that your this attitude may spoil your present. If you are not able to shape your present then mind it, you will not be able to achieve your future.

The great achievers of this world who desired to enjoy their future they strictly preferred to live in present. They did to best shape their present so as to fully enjoy it. They better understood that it would be the present only which will make their future worth enjoying. You are so involved and content with your work and it so happens that fame comes to you. That's nice, if it does not, no problem. For you fame is no way any pre-condition for what you do. Otherwise you will not be able to develop the feel the way you want to. You need to enjoy whatever you are doing with deep sustenance. The name and fame would automatically follow.

In the materialistic world of today the social attitude has largely become money oriented. People are seen running restless after money either this way or that. They even go on unhesitant resorting to all unlawful means to earn money. This in fact is a kind of lust. The entire objective to enjoy life gets hampered. It has become very common that people spoil their health for earning money. Then they are seen wasting all their money so earned in hospitals for earning good health. Now the big question is what is left behind for you to enjoy with? Whether good health or the money? By the time it is too late. Absolutely choice is of yours and of none else. There should not be any doubt about it. You always wish to enjoy your life. Every person does. It is up to you only to ensure to enjoy what you do? And you do such things or works so that you are able to enjoy. That's it.

I totally agree with your view point that today's world has become completely materialistic. Where one needs to survive in such world then money becomes the basic factor. For big social and economic status people earn money. This is the way that they learn to enjoy their life. I do not say that earning money in life is not important. But what I mean to be important is the method and the means people resort to earn money? There is a vast difference between the hard earned money by lawful means and off course the easy earned money by resorting to unlawful means. Now it would be the choice of a human being to choose either of the two means to earn money and link with it as to which give him comparatively the better kind of pleasure to enjoy with?

Set of people can make a kind of pleas that merely earning money itself is a pleasure for them. It is immaterial whether what means are adopted to earn that money. Money itself begets pleasure. That's it. They are very boldly heard making such statements that they can buy any kind of pleasure find on this earth with the help of money. Every enjoyment of life is well within their reach. That is their way of enjoying life. They do not care for all that. Ambitions of life could be fulfilled with the help of money. There would be hardly any problem to shape the future. Money makes it all possible within moments. So why to bother about all that which is absolutely unnecessary in the present materialistic world? Yes…!!!... One has to ensure to enjoy what he does. Becoming money oriented is not bad particularly when you are working hard to earn money in an absolutely honest manner. It must be heavenly pleasure that you have earned huge wealth by your caliber, merit and hard work. You are extending your helping hand too to the needy poor people in your society. Oh…!!!... That is great. This is not materialism by any standard. Sharing one's part of wealth to the people who are in need is spiritual in true sense.

It is a difficult task for a person to part with his money to any other person who is not so related to him. One can judge the mental level of such man who so decides to help others. He is utilizing his material for a novel cause. He has got the objective in his life where the materialistic tendency does not come in his way in any manner. He will be the healthiest person on this earth and would be enjoying his deeds in a most satisfactory manner. But count of such philanthropists is very less in number on this earth. Some go for charity so as to balance their accounts. But they would not be able to enjoy what they do since they adopt this trick to escape the clutches of law. This off course would not be spiritual albeit some people in need are served upon. Enjoying what we do is strictly personal in the sense that you earn first. At the same time earning only is not all that for a better spiritual life. What becomes material is that you enjoy what you earn. If you are not able to enjoy your earnings then give a serious thought to it. You may earn less but could enjoy most. It is though difficult but possible when you develop a kind of mastery that you do not fall slave to your material. Come forward to enjoy your life the way you like it.

"In the materialistic world of today the social attitude has largely become money oriented. People are seen running restless after money either this way or that. They even go on unhesitant resorting to all unlawful means to earn money. This in fact is a kind of lust. The entire objective to enjoy life gets hampered. It has become very common that people spoil their health for earning

money. Then they are seen wasting all their money so earned in hospitals for earning good health. Now the big question is what is left behind for you to enjoy with? Whether good health or the money? By the time it is too late."

———————————————————

9

AT PEACE WITH NATURE

What do we mean by peace with nature? This question becomes more significant when we say it to be our 'mother nature'. Every one respects the mother so is the situation with the 'mother nature'. Do we need to be at peace with our mother? How come such situations arise? If there are situations which do not look like to be at peace with mother then really it is much disturbing? The big question we encounter with today whether we are at peace with nature? Why does this question arise at all? We are bound to feel that we are not at peace. We should imagine for disasters if we are not at peace with 'mother nature' and keep disturbing it. We are facing disasters and other natural calamities on regular intervals giving rise to huge loss of life and property all across the globe proving conclusively to the fact that all is not well between the people and the 'mother nature'.

The philosophy behind being in peace with nature is very complicated. Look for the peace to prevail in skies. Let the peace prevail on this earth too. The peace in flowing rivers would be boon for the mankind. We can perceive peace in the plants, the trees and the animals then imagine the kind of natural balance on this earth. The peace in the vast space would be unparallel. Do we have the courage to assess about the damage we have done to the nature? Do not hesitate. Let us come forward to take responsibility for all the degradation caused to our environment. The natural habitat and ecosystem for living beings has been destroyed by us. We are polluting our soil, water and the air. Depleting ozone layer is the consequence we are coming across closely followed by climatic imbalance in the form of global warming at one extreme and global cooling to the other extreme.

It is a matter of grave concern as to how do we feel about the nature and also the sense to preserve and protect the nature? It should be the feel for our nature which is full of purity, beauty, tranquility and peace. What the Almighty has created for the mankind to survive with are millions of living organisms the flora and fauna, beautiful landscapes, seas, rivers, mountains, deserts, forests and the plains. It is absolutely criminal if man is found to be destroying the nature. If natural disasters follow as a consequence of such destructions then who is to be blamed for it? We only and none else...!!! How can the nature be at peace under these circumstances? All the negligence and the greed perpetuated by the human agency on this earth. Let us not forget the laws of nature. It does not spare the one who goes on to play with it mercilessly. Let us admit this very fact that economic developments are being pursued all around the world at the cost of ecological preservation. The world is fast becoming more vulnerable to natural disasters and we only are to be blamed for all destructions. We should always remember that we are an integral part of nature. It must always be our pious obligation to preserve and protect the environment and establish peace with the nature on earth.

Why there is hue and cry all around that we are not at peace with our 'mother nature'? We need to ask to our inner conscience that whether we have given serious thought to this problem? We immediately start considering it to be a 'problem' only when we sense that there appears to be a 'risk' to our lives. Otherwise we remain least bothered about it. How strange, 'mother nature' is going to be a 'problem' for us? Unbelievable...!!! Unthinkable...!!! Who is responsible for creating this situation? Why do we forget that the mother earth nurtures our life by flowing through our arteries and the veins? What the kind of 'problem' could we have with our mother earth? That the kind of risk to our life? No...no...!!! The nature could never think so. Oh...!!! Nature is the life giver to us exactly the way a 'mother' is the life giver to living beings. Why our rivers are getting short of water? And are getting dried up gradually and gradually? What will happen after a due course of time when people on this earth would fight for water with each other? Is there anyone to address these issues? Very soon water resources on earth would be lesser whereas demand for water would go much higher? Our so called 'conscious people' who suppose them to be 'responsible one' have started visualizing the possibilities of a World War-III, only for the sake of water. They should be ready to quench their 'thirst' by yet another 'Blood War'. They suppose that they would win since they are stronger. They do not seem to be serious enough to look for possibilities to prevent wastage of water and save water but simply attending to conferences and summits coming out with formal resolutions with no executions. But...!!!...Yes...!!! They would be ready to go on waging war, killing innocent lives, and shedding blood for the sake of water. They forget that scarcity of water on this earth would destroy the flora and fauna too. The drought as a result would burn the forests and the entire vegetation useful for survival of life on earth. When there is no oxygen in the atmosphere due to destruction of vegetation and forests then who will remain on this earth to see as to how many of us are left behind? Moving around carrying with oxygen cylinders on shoulders is not going to be the 'ultimate solution'.

Why do we fail to observe the raining patterns in our modern times? The raining pattern is on decreasing trend year after the year. I used to read in my childhood that forests and vegetations are very essential for good rains. In the name of development forests are being cut mercilessly and vegetations are being destroyed. We are blindly heading for manmade destructions. We often hear our planners who suggest rain harvesting for water conservation. How ridiculous? Where are the rains to harvest for? No doubt our world has advanced much in science and technology but only to compete with the nature. There needs to be serious and honest debate on whether the science has contributed to the nature? Or else...!!! It has exploited the nature? Why do we fail to understand that science would not be able to replenish the nature which has already been exploited a lot? Please...!!! Do not argue that it is all for the sake of development. It is for whom sake? Is it for the sake of mankind? How come? And the mankind is already made to approach gradually towards the verge of destruction. 'Mother Nature' would never think even in her distant dreams that its 'generations' are so destroyed by their own suicidal acts. How could she be able to help us when we do go beyond her control by our mischievous acts or omissions? We do not listen to her calls at all. Our 'mother nature' appears to be badly tired now by our omissions. We do not have any sense of feeling towards her sentiments. This is criminal by all standards so we should keep ready to face the music. Let us not oblige the 'mother nature' by caring to her sentiments.

What do we expect from our 'mother nature'? Kindly ask to your inner conscience if you do have one at all. What the 'mother nature' expects from us all? She never expects anything from us. Why should she? She only gives and bestows her blessings to her children. It would be criminal if you are expecting something from your 'mother nature' at the cost of destroying her. It is her 'motherhood' that she must be worried about your wellness on this earth. Do not leave your mother to be merely a silent spectator for your ill motivated deeds against nature. It is self suicidal. You have failed in your duty to protect and conserve your 'mother nature'. You have rendered her absolutely handicapped. You have snatched her peace of mind and she is not keeping well. Why to make you aware about your duties? Even if your duties are made known to you it is certain that you will remain least bothered about it as your past misdeeds so indicate. Mother will keep caring for you to the extent possible despite the fact that you keep ignoring her. Kindly get peace for her for the sake of your own self. May be you are not going to do that since you are for development. But still please…!!! Do it. Mother is waiting for you to be at peace with you.

Amidst my getting ready with this book the novel virus Covid-19 has knocked at the doors of world communities letting them feel realize that they are not at peace with nature. They are charged with indiscriminate exploitation of nature, its flora and fauna, extreme disturbance of its ecological balance and the biological diversity. Every time the advocates of development would come forward dismissing the charges as baseless. They would justify by all unreasonable means that development is for the mankind. My argument under the circumstances would be that developmental activities have their own specified limits. Major countries need to understand that developments can never be unlimited and should not be permitted at the cost of survival of the mankind on this earth. Nature would explode the moment its balancing mechanisms are destroyed by our wrong doings. The kind of explosion the world is witnessing today in the form of Covid-19 pandemics that till the First week of May 2020 it has already claimed more than 2,42,000 deaths all across more than 185 nations with more than 34lacs people reported to be suffering from the novel virus. The World Health Organization (WHO) is scared about that this number may further increase in coming days. The writings on the wall are crystal clear. Either the world should learn and repent honestly or keep ready to be vanished. I would repeat again that 'Mother Nature' would never think even in her distant dreams that its 'generations' are so destroyed by their own suicidal acts. Nature has to balance itself so are the sufferings for our own wrongful deeds. Nature always leaves a space behind for us to repent and withdraw from where we cross our limits. We would win the battle with Covid-19 ultimately but with a huge loss of life and shattered world economy. The lesson we are going to learn from this pandemic should last long in our memories and the generations to come that playing with nature would be disastrous again and again.

"Look for the peace to prevail in the skies. Let the peace prevail on this earth too. The peace in flowing rivers would be boon for the mankind. We can perceive peace in the plants, the trees and the animals then imagine the kind of natural balance on this earth. The peace in the vast space would be unparallel. Do we have the courage to assess about the damage we have already done to the nature? Do not hesitate. Let us come forward to take responsibility for all the degradation caused to our environment. The natural habitat and ecosystem for living beings has been destroyed by us. We are polluting our soil, water and the air."

10

LIFE ACTION PLAN

It is very essential for every individual to draw a life action plan and then seriously work upon it for a better life. Consciously or unconsciously we all draw up a life action plan for a systematic and peaceful life. We need to understand 'geography' of our life. For the purpose of controlling and regulating the earth system the nature develops its own geographical conditions. In a similar manner for governing our life properly we need to develop geographical conditions of our own body system. Geographical conditions are important for maintaining ecological balancing of human body. Our body has its own well developed 'ecosystem' which plays a very significant role in human life. Ecosystem of our body could be understood in terms of 'bio-chemical' relationships within human body.

We are able to prepare life action plan in due conformity with bio-chemistry our body and mind. Physical soundness of our body is in fact actual understanding of human bio-chemistry as to what is happening through our nervous system, blood circulatory system, digestive system in our body. Any disturbance with bio-chemistry of our body system quickly makes an impact on our body and mind. This impact may generate joyful impact and also an impact full with sorrow. Bio-chemical impact full with happiness or sorrow would be depending upon the nature of impulses a person is feeling in the form of positive and negative emotions. We do share these emotions with the people we are in relationship. We may be extrovert or introvert in maintaining such relationship further in our life. We come across certain relationships which are made subject to various conditions. May be we are not in a position to fulfill those conditions.

I do believe that conditional relationships damage your life action plans because people do not realize your priorities and are more self-centered. These are the testing times for a person when he needs to firmly pursue his action plans without bothering for the people who go on to break conditional relationships. If your emotions are not being honored by those who are in relationship with you then how long you would be in position to strain your emotions and feelings? No matter. Draw your life action plan in such a manner that your pious objectives in your life are not put to any sort of compromise. Make it a point that one or two stronger relations are much valuable than hundred weak relations. Human memory is very neutral in the sense that it stores memories within it both of the good times as well as of the bad times. Our life action plan should strictly prefer for the good ones so that we are more comfortable with bad ones. You cannot completely rub off your bad memories from your mind but with the help of your life action you can nicely make a balancing between the two. This way our life moves on smoothly and perfectly.

The trouble moments in our life adversely affect our life action plan. Our troubles may be of psychological, physical or economic nature. The question must be that why after all such troubles cropped up? Is it the case that our troubles were results of our wrongful life action plan? Why a man would commit any such error or wrong unless he was absolutely forced to do so by certain compelling circumstances? This is the very natural question which comes to mind. Or do we commit wrongs out of mere innocence? Our social or economic troubles could be born out of social circumstances but the psychological troubles are basically individual. But it is also not like that the social and economic state of a man does not influence his psychology or way of thinking. Yes…!!! It does. Social and economic backwardness of a nation would definitely put an adverse impact on the mental state of its citizens. Comprehensive positive thinking of citizens of a poor nation advances when such nation is in a position to win over its poverty conditions. Are the compelling situations and circumstances not within the control of a man or even the state? How could a man control poverty and backwardness? In poverty conditions the man is not even able to fill his empty stomach or his family members by getting food. First he gets the strength of food then he may think of any control. How could a man then be able to draw his life action plan? There could be no doubt about it that poverty renders a man psychologically weak. Such a psyche has been directly linked with physical weakness of the man. How could the life of such man be full with happiness? Then talking about life action plan would appear to be of no meaning. Disturbed 'bio-chemistry' of such people would become a permanent part in their life process. Making life action plan for such people would be no priority rather than to survive first on this earth.

For a nation every citizen of its society is significant. The happiness of a nation's citizens could undoubtedly be the scale to measure wellness of that nation. Why any nation would not intend to be a good planner for its citizen and think of the need for the people in helping them making action plan of their life? One may talk about to move life in an unplanned manner and making life roaming around without any direction. Could he be then able to achieve the objectives of his life? Planning is always for betterment. At the time of planning we need to first identify our weaknesses and also our areas of strength. It would be significant for the purpose of proper balancing between the two. Weaknesses for us are quite inherent but a good planning helps in minimizing its negative impacts. Where he has worked upon his plans honestly he has been successful. There have been great people on this earth whose life action plan had been not for personal gain but for human welfare. They were never self centered and acted upon their plans sincerely. They never restricted themselves to their national boundaries and went beyond it execute their life action plan to help out the mankind. Their life action plan included all such people on the whole earth in need of help. What made them 'great' on this earth was the execution part of their plan which needs indeed an untiring effort. They were not ordinary people and their greatness lies in the fact itself that they did not live for themselves. Their life has been for the welfare of others only. Why can't we ordinary people make a life action plan at least for ourselves and work upon it sincerely?

Our states are in the role of 'welfare state'. The state has enough resources at its disposal. It must be the obligation of the state to help out their citizen in making out their life action plan according to their need. Where states come out with determined steps then definitely they would be able to do all that what is needful in execution of life action plan of a man. For many their life action plan has been just to fulfill their basic minimum needs. That's it. What else? They want nothing more but just bread to eat, clothes to cover their naked body and a roof for shelter, family health and proper education to their children. They wish to happily carry out their life's liabilities and then peaceful life departure from this earth. Nothing more than it could be life action plan of an individual. That's all not small things for such a long life's struggle for majority of people on this earth who are not able to plan their action for the reasons of depravity. How our states would be able to digest this bitter truth that even today billions of people on this earth are forced to live empty stomach? What do we expect from such hungry people that the kind of their life action plan would be? Are they in a position even to give a thought about their life action plan? Their life existence itself is at stake. If they are able to save their lives then they will see to it. Where even a single individual goes to sleep without food then it is shameful and should be a matter of serious concern for an ideal state. But why should we imagine such an ideal state after all? When our states turn blind eyes and start indulging in 'politics' then they tend to forget about their duties. My humble submission would be that whenever you sit to prepare your life action plan kindly leave some space within it so that the man around you gets some help from you. He is the one who was not able to make his life action plan for multiple societal reasons and went disappointed. My friends...!!! This would be your great life action plan in your life. Salutes...!!!

"For many their life action plan has been just to fulfill their basic minimum needs. That's it. What else? They want nothing

more but just bread to eat, clothes to cover their naked body and roof for shelter, family health and proper education to their children. They wish to happily carry out their life's liabilities and peaceful life departure from this earth. Nothing more than it could be the life action plan for an individual".

11

NEVER FEAR OF UNCERTAINTY

Uncertainty in your life some way or the other is bound to be there around. If minutely observed uncertainties are not to be feared but it motivates a person to struggle. That should be the reason to think upon it sensibly since we struggle in life as we fear about our uncertain future. We dream for an ambitious future and so follow our action. An action motivated by our ambitions should not be considered to be antithesis to the law of action. Law of action is an extreme philosophy for 'karma' where there should be no desire for results. If we are honest towards our karma results would follow appropriately. We begin our action with big future dream in our mind. Why not...??? We should have a dream. We should have a goal to target. Problem arises when we become so involved with it that we wish to achieve the goal at any cost. This extreme feeling to achieve infuses suffering through negative emotions particularly under the circumstances when we undertake actions for results to happen. We know it fully well those results are beyond our control. We can control our actions by putting in continuous hard work. But how can we control the results in our favor? No doubt getting desired results is the source of happiness for the mankind. In the event of unfavorable outcome disappointment leads to despair. This is not good for human psychology and makes a man to fear with. Oh...!!! What is this? Why this disappointment for not being successful? This is not the end of your world. We have to do a lot in our life. After all sky is the limit. You have never to disappoint as you possess unlimited potential to fly even beyond the skies.

It is human weakness that we start action with strong belief that whatever we think or dream it will come true provided we work hard. But it so happens that despite hard working we fail to get the desired results. Yes...!!! It happens. We should not forget that outcome of every action is controlled by forces of the universe which are not within our means. We come across obstacles at the same time there are moments of encouragement too. We need to capture these moments in the form of right opportunities at the right point of time. We are not alert and miss these moments. We feel fear of uncertainty and a tendency of disappointment only for the reasons that we have the outcome in mind. The fear is of not reaching the goals or getting the ambitions not fulfilled. The law of universe is very unique. If the things do not materialize the way you planned then make it a point in your mind that the universe has a different plan of action for you. Be confident that your action will not go waste anyway. You have a determined role to play in this universe. Keep ready for that. You are only the actor director is the universe. You will feel the difference yourself when you perform action with a sense of duty rather then you are passionate for a desired fruit of action. Always be certain that you have to perform honestly and forget about uncertainty. You will not be then feared of uncertainties. You will ultimately be the real achiever.

What do you make out the meaning of uncertainty? Why don't you consider that it is quite natural a thing in our life? Had everything been certain then nothing has been left behind for us to do? We would not work hard left leave making honest efforts and would sit idle considering that such happening was certain. Keep this positive side of uncertainty in your mind that this too has its own philosophy. It is humbly requested that natural certainties please be not seen with reference to human uncertainties. Where, there is life, death is certain. It would be certainty that the sun rises in the east and sets in the west direction. Nights followed by days would be certain. Sun light would be hot while moon light would be pleasant. Seasons would come and go on a certain pattern. Rivers would emerge and finally meet with the sea. Did we ever look to this very fact that how the certainties of nature are so accurate? Why the human references are not that certain and accurate? That's the point in fact. Nature's uncertainty means a gone case. World is compelled to confess with a guilty feel that human factor has rendered this nature to be uncertain leading towards end of life on this earth. Rules of nature are very hard. But still nature ensures to follow its rules to be certain. Any such rules which are natural are not hard, what is hard is to regularly follow up those rules. This only is the big difference between 'natural certainty' and 'human uncertainty'. For example, there is a rule like the person leaves the bed at five o'clock in the morning. The person is said to move with nature. Do we consider it to be a hard rule? Can't a person leave his bed regularly at five in the morning? This rule appears to be very easy. Then we should be in a position to ensure to follow up this rule in similarly easy manner. But we are not able to do this since the person is not able to leave his bed at five in the morning. This easy appearing rule proves to be hard one rendering our life uncertain. This way starts uncertainties of persons. The secrets of natural certainties are hidden in those regular follow ups of the hard rules of the nature. Why can't we follow them up? It is as simple as that.

Uncertainty definitely scares a person. For getting a certain future we need to remove our uncertainty. Make some hard rules for you and ensure to follow them on regular basis. You will see that now you are not scared of uncertainties in your life. We should examine this fact as to why, after all, we come across uncertainties in our life? We were not honest in our conduct to follow the rules sincerely. Philosophically the law of action in our life is the procedural stage of following rules of life. It is for this reason the law of action makes specific declaration if the person performs his actions sincerely then he would certainly get the fruits of his actions. The certainty of getting results means removal of uncertainties from the life of the person. Think to be ambitious and fulfill them at any cost of your positive efforts. To achieve things at any cost means the determination to demand certainty. But the conditions would be that whether we did follow the secrets of natural certainty? Your life would no more be uncertain.

Why should we human get hopeless after all? There are precedents in the history of human achievements that even after regular honest efforts a person could not be successful. Uncertainties disappoint him but he never lost his hope. He was not getting desired results. Negative feelings used to make room within his mind. He was not ready to accept the defeat. He was not ready to surrender and sit tired. His firm determination never left him alone. He swears that he has to achieve success in his life. It became possible due to the laws of action that his determination was imbibed in his arteries and veins. Why would such man be scared of uncertainties? He has now reached such a stage of human psychology that he would frame new definitions of human certainties. Man made troubles would be created for him. People would start addressing him that he has gone mad. Such negativity would discourage him on every step. When the person goes determined the negative acts and troubles created by others would make him stronger from within. The man would emerge successful. People would still continue with their negative acts. Now this would now no way affect the man. The man would feel pity about them and would be ready to excuse them.

Make it a point that worldly forces would predetermine your role subject to the conditions the efforts you are putting in sincerely. Then you will be prepared to emerge in that role from within to deal with such situations. You will now be psychologically strong enough to not to be scared of uncertainties around you. You will be subjected to kind of uncertainties by the worldly forces so that you are properly trained and are able to win over. Then you will see that achievements become day to day habit for you. It should be regular feature as how you take uncertainties of your life and in what shape? Once you are able to command you will able to shape them as well. One who fears struggle is bound to be scared of life's uncertainties he should then forget to think of to be successful. Remember that to win is within your nature exploit it. You need to learn sincerely to bring it out.

"It is human weakness that we start action with strong belief that whatever we think or dream it will come true provided we work hard. But it so happens that despite hard working we fail to get the desired results. Yes…!!! It happens. We should not forget that outcome of every action is controlled by the forces of universe which is not within our means. We come across obstacles at the same time there are moments of encouragements too. We need to capture these moments in the form of right opportunities at the right point of time. We are not alert and miss these moments."

12

UNIVERSE OF THE MIND

Despite the fact that we are the creatures of the universe but our mind has the magic capacity to create its own universe. Our mind is the unique gift of the universe. It is said that the knowledge is power and off course it is. Mind generates knowledge and on the basis of that knowledge it creates lot of realities in life, the reality of being a human and the reality of being universe. Mind is responsible to unearth the truth about existence of human beings and the universe all around. Human beings are for the human beings so they must be for human beings. Mind is the centre point which determines through generations that what should be the universal revolutionary path for ultimate advancement of mankind on this earth? It is only the perfection of mind which will make the search for right advancement of the universe in right direction what the civilizations are looking for in present times.

What has gone wrong with the universe and the mind as well? Are we not thinking rightly and having a mind with no prejudice? Why there are sufferings for mankind on this earth? Generations still suffer from socio-economic backwardness, living below poverty line, ill health, malnutrition, low quality education, struggling for their basic minimum survival needs. What has gone wrong with the generating knowledge power of the mind? Universe possesses in itself the whole nature, human beings, animals, flora and fauna. Conclusion is that it is the human mind which is accountable for pollution of environment its degradation and ecological imbalance. Polluted thinking is also responsible for imbalance of the universe in the shape of socio-economic disruption on this earth. We need to reconstruct the universe keeping this fact in mind that every person is born equal. The practice of prevalent socio-economic inequality could only be eliminated from this universe if we are ready to take steps towards right evolution with a participatory mind. Let us not forget that mind is central to every process we put forward, every phenomenon and the evolutionary trends which affect the mankind in its march for betterment. Thinking processes of participatory minds possess magical potency to create its own universe. It not only renders the healing touch to the polluted mind but also inculcates in the sense of quality and virtues. Mind has the strength to mould things in a strict positive direction and the same could be carefully utilized for the sake of the mankind.

With the advancement of civilizations world psychologists feel that we have such minds in this universe which have proved to be more than a 'social animal'. What we now need is the universal participation of such minds. Such minds would create a new universe packed with equitable socio-economic situations full with happiness and life on this earth.

There is universe in the form of physical existence of living or non-living things. Human mind has its own universe and the kind of thinking process. At times thinking of men breaks all limits and goes to the extent of destroying the boundaries of the universe. Human mind has the miraculous capacity to think and work upon getting destructive and constructive too at the same time. Whenever, it thinks destructively then it goes dangerous for the universe. Human mind has been working for decades and goes completely destructive to unleash nuclear and chemical warfare. What for and what to achieve with? Out to destroy civilizations and kill its own fellow human beings. Bloodshed…!!! Arguments are always made that nuclear energy will be utilized for peaceful purposes only. But credibility of such arguments is doubted when such nuclear powers start making threatening calls for nuclear warfare against each other. How foolish it is? There are reported instances that countries have used chemical weapons to terrorize their enemies and establish their supremacy. Use of nuclear or chemical weapons would not be end of it but it would prove to be beginning of all that destruction all across the globe.

Strength of human mind is superb so is the universe of the mind. All such strengths should always be considered for betterment of the humanity and its prosperity on this earth. Universal peace strengthens human bonds whereas breach of peace not only weakens it but permanently destroys the bonds of humanity. It is because of their thinking patterns and mental strength men claim to be better from animal existence. But their claim appears to be absolutely fake and bogus when they are seen fighting worst than animals. They should never forget that it would be defeat of the human mind if they fail to achieve the very objectives behind the origin of the mankind on this earth. The universe of the human mind should search for the ways and means to establish brotherhood among the human beings rather than to spread hatred among them. The history of the mankind on this earth reveals to the fact that the human tendency after the human blood has been for the reasons that the human mind intended to rule and to establish its supremacy over the others. The way they could think was that they would kill, they would destroy and they would rule.

Socio-economic disparity on this earth has been due to the result of polluted thinking of human minds. For a healthy and prosperous universal community on this earth the human minds need to give a serious thought over the issue that it is not the tendency of destruction but it is the policy of construction only which would ultimately help the mankind to survive with human dignity. There should be no reason for men to establish their supremacy over one another. Why should after all? How commendable it would be if men feel realize the sentiments of other men even if the other happens to be inferior one? Human bonding could be strong and essential which no force can break even. What a man would require other than his basic minimum daily needs for the sake of his survival? This goes without saying that it should be a matter of serious concern for the human minds to concentrate and think upon that in the modern world of today majority of people are seen struggling for fulfillment of their basic minimum needs even. But they are not able to get as per their needs they fail and are destined to die of starvation. A single death due to hunger is a big black spot on the human mind whereas the world witnesses starvation deaths in mass in different corners of the globe. This is an utter defeat of the universe of the mind where it absolutely failed to protect even the basic minimum interests of its fellow human beings.

Participatory mind is central to the human development where every mind should have a scope to participate with and work upon the human development policies. Why there should be a tendency of someone to be rulers and a majority to be ruled upon? Why think to deprive of someone or to destroy? Won't this reflect to be worst than an animal tendency? Why then we claim ourselves to be superior to animals? This is not a positive universe of mind. Our past has been testimony to this very fact that the world has not changed its tendency and thinking patterns toward our fellow human beings. Why don't we admit that our claim to be a superior mind has been absolutely fake and bogus? My humble submission is that we need to stop and think for a moment till we reach to the point of no return. The universe of the human mind has an abundant capacity to think and then work upon it for a better human development provided that it starts with and keeps thinking honestly and without any prejudice of any kind against its fellow human beings. Thinking supreme about inferiors is the supremacy of the mind in true sense. Possibilities of hope are always there within the universe of human mind. Thinking supreme only would not be sufficient unless it is translated into policy initiatives and implemented sincerely at the grass roots levels. If the benefits of such mind initiatives do not reach to the needy then entire exercise would be just an eye wash. Let the world always remember that thinking supreme costs nothing but being supreme matters for the development of the mankind. Think big. Think great.

"The universe of the human mind should search for the ways and means to establish brotherhood among the human beings rather than to spread hatred among them. The history of the mankind

on this earth reveals to the fact that the human tendency after the human blood has been for the reasons that the human mind intended to rule and to establish its supremacy over the others. The way they could think was that they would kill, they would destroy and they would rule."

13

MORALITY OF SECULARISM

People are heard saying on number of occasions that it is very difficult to define the term secularism. But to my understanding if we see the term secularism with an open mind and practice it without any prejudice then it becomes very easy to define it. It is as simple as understanding about oneself and understanding about a child. The practices which are just and fair in any society are simply to be termed as secular. Any societal conduct which is fairly right and logical comes within the ambit of secular conduct and such practices should be terms as of secular character. Why it becomes that difficult to define this term? It is only because of the reason that we are not just and fair in our actions so we fail to practice it. We act arbitrarily and discriminate among people around us. The moment we violate the principles of natural justness and fairness we fail to be secular.

Should we consider fundamental freedom to religious belief as secularism? Whether this freedom also includes not professing any religion whatsoever? What could be the morality of secularism? The freedom of religion advocates for freedom of choice to profess any religion of your likings. Morality of secularism prohibits any kind of religious intervention into due and just human conduct and fair collective societal behavior. It has been observed that religious interventions have been source of divisiveness and inequality among various communities and are responsible for inter religious conflicts for centuries. Even in the modern world such conflicts have become very common. There is no doubt about it that all the existing religions provide for moral code of conduct to its followers which may be felt necessary in any contemporary society. There are codes of conduct which are regulated by the collective conscience of the people with full honesty and sincerity which possess virtual secularist tenets and become of universal acceptability and application. Practicing of being honest, non-violent, truthfulness, to be fair, love for the mankind, character building, utmost integrity, are the strong foundations of being secular.

Religious diversity must not be seen as differential. It must be given universal acceptance with a sense of mutual respect to all the religions and also to its believers. The non-believers also render service to the mankind in their own way of thinking and by their secular approach to worldly affairs. The complexity of thought in projecting any particular religion being superior religion among others creates all the problems. Such projections of being superior are completely unwarranted considering to the fact that all persons are born equal on this earth without any identity of either their caste or community. Based upon the principles of equality, justness and fairness secularism would never permit any social or political system to be divisive and sectarian. Those who think and act for the common good and do not work for their narrow personal gains are the humanistic people with realistic secular character in true sense. Secularism should not be equated with a concept to be discussed along with existing religious considerations. Secularism reigns above the religions and even beyond which is in search of the eternal truth for welfare of the mankind, to establish equality among the human beings on this earth irrespective of their caste and creed so that they can live with human dignity. Justness and fairness would automatically follow once equality is established without any sign of discrimination. This only is the morality of secularism.

As has been mentioned earlier alternatively secularism has to be studied by connecting it from any particular religion. Talking about religious secularism means any society or nation being secular affording its citizen liberty to profess any religion of their choice. Non secular states go for a nationally sponsored religion to be practiced by its citizen. There being a compulsion to follow any particular religion or there being a liberty to not to believe in any of the religions. My humble submission is that let there is any number of religions after all what is going to be the morality of any religion? If we talk about humanity beyond religions then we would come across a very simple question that whether on this earth humanity came into existence first or the religions? Obviously similarly simple would be the reply of this question that first humanity only came into existence on this earth then came the religions. Different religions or religious faiths are the codes for controlling and regulating the human conduct. Where human conduct may be towards a particular individual, living beings or towards the nature, human feelings should clearly reflect into it. Do we not have sufficient ground before us to consider this fact that the religions some way or the other is manmade? Where is a religion which would not talk about welfare of the humanity or protection of human interests? Whether any such religion or human code of conduct would talk about violation of humanity? All the religions which exist on this earth today would never allow any violation of humanity. Sources of different religions provide us divine touch and the divine feeling. Why don't we see the divine look direct in our fellow human beings? Religions do confer in them the divinity for us to realize with.

There should be argument on the point that whether there is any statutory compulsion to relate secularism with one religion or the other? Whether to be secular do we need to take the cover of any religion? In what reference secularism should be understood? We would be said to be secular when we would stop discriminate among human beings. We would be secular when we are helping a needy one as per our capacity. We are secular when we are not going fanatic in the name of religion. We undertook initiatives to eradicate poverty of the people who are poor. We use to make efforts to see that their children did not sleep empty stomach. Constitutions of world admit this very fact that situations of disparity existed among people in the society. There are lot many evidences available that world governments encouraged tendencies of disparity so that they can divide and rule. Let such disparities be in the form of religious beliefs, caste based, color of skin i.e. apartheid or the rich and the poor. Discrimination between haves and have notes, who have no fresh air to breath, no bread to eat and water to fill up their empty stomach. Had it been that easy to define the morality of secularism then probably all would have been well in this world? Be sure all is not well and needs your sincere attention.

Why don't we get the way which takes us to our destination? Our destination could not be different than the human welfare. The various streams of religions too ultimately terminate at the point of human welfare only. Then why the very human existence is at stake when human welfare is in the center of all religions? The morality of secularism lies in the fact that different religions should come forward with an authentic reply to this question. Risk to human existence means a question mark into the reliability of various religious faiths. Morality of secularism lies in the establishment of human peace and overall peace and tranquility on this earth. Let that be any religion there are genuine reasons to be worried about as to what do we mean by religious fanaticism? If religions do not permit fanaticism then such occurrences on different parts of this earth become more worrisome and unfortunate. We only would have to take positive initiatives towards establishment of static human peace. It would be possible with unbiased respect and developing of mutual trust with each other. That's what we are lacking in today. We are not honest to our conducts. There is always a big question mark on our reliability as to what we say and what we do. We do fail in keeping our words. We should not keep any false expectation that one day some angel would come down from skies and set the things right on this earth. It is not going to happen unless we are ready to make serious move. Things would be alright but on the conditions of our own honest initiatives. The secularity of human life lies in the fact that its beauty should be visible in its totality to each and every individual on this earth irrespective of their religion, caste or creed.

"Religious diversity must not be seen as differential. It must be given universal acceptance with a sense of mutual respect to all the religions and also to its believers. The non-believers also

render service to the mankind in the same manner in their own way of thinking and by secular approach to the worldly affairs. The complexity of thoughts in projecting any particular religion being superior religion among others creates all the problems. Such projections of being superior are completely unwarranted considering to the fact that all persons are born equal on this earth without any identity of either their caste or community".

———————————————

14

ATTAINMENT OF NIRVANA

Attainment of nirvana has direct relationship with spiritual enlightenment of a person. We get sufficient material relating to 'nirvana' under Buddhist philosophy. Power of human imaginations plays a very significant role in virtual realization of human realities on this earth. Who will acknowledge the sacredness of all the life and related worldly phenomenon? Human sufferings are the noble truths of life. Who will feel realize the suffering as a mental condition? The person himself would who happens to suffer the pain. People may express their lip sympathy for human sufferings but they cannot share them individually. The doctor may attend to help cure the sufferings from pain but he would not give any guarantee for permanent relief. The pain may recur as it arises out of an individual mental condition.

Do we correlate nirvana as freedom from worldly affairs? Do we attain nirvana only after death? How good it could be when we are able to attain nirvana during our lifetime and we live with it? There are sufferings in life that is true. Do you think that you will get freedom from your sufferings only after your death? No...!!! It is not like that. Your mind is sufficiently capable to handle sufferings in your lifetime and also to live with it. How to handle sufferings is not a big task. It is as simple as you could imagine. Think well, do good, speak well, and listen well, see well, that's it. It is up to us only to examine our inner self whether what induces us to think bad or speak bad? Once we are in the process of thinking bad resultantly we are bound to speak bad or do bad. You only can speculate within yourself about your deeds. When the nature has bestowed you the power of self-speculation then why do you fail in it? May be we are reckless and do not bother about our inner self. Make it a point then we are inviting sufferings for our own self. We just cannot escape from it. No one should be blamed for our self induced sufferings. Achievement of complete nirvana during your life time goes with your attitude and the mindset. Attain nirvana by the strength of your mind. Never allow others to play with your mind. It reflects your mental weakness. If you are continuing in such a state of mind being disturbed by others, it would give permanency to your mindset. It would be very easy for others to keep disturbing you. Attainment of nirvana would remain a mirage for you during your life time. May be you are able to get it only after your death but you are not able to feel it or enjoy it.

Here this point would also be very essential to understand that what is the kind of mutual relationship between attainment of nirvana and freedom from sins? What is the definition of sin? You are scared of sin but still you are indulging in sin. Hurting sentiments of somebody would come within the ambit of sin. Here hurting sentiments would be a small thing people are ready to go to the extent of committing culpable homicides. Not innocently but intentionally with all due knowledge and preparedness. Human being inflicting pain to another human being is nothing but creation of his mind. Is it an indication of healthy mind? Researches reveal that people derive pleasure by inflicting pain to others. How come then inflicting minds would remain calm and healthy? One fails to understand how come such minds enjoy pleasure out of inflicting pains? If the person could not get nirvana during his lifetime then who has seen it that he would get it after he is dead? There are talks of fore birth i.e. life before life. It is said that the person would not have done good deeds in his fore birth so his sufferings. He would have committed sins in his earlier birth that is why he is suffering of the sins in this birth. If the person has to suffer the punishment of the sins of his fore birth in his rebirth then where is the nirvana. If you kept suffering of the sins of fore birth then when is the time for you to be able to do some good deeds so as to improve your rebirth? It goes without saying that your human birth has gone a complete waste.

What could be the philosophy of fore birth? Whether human gets rebirth after his death? One would achieve nirvana only after he gets freedom from sins. If during his lifetime a person commits sins then would he be able to get nirvana in this life time? For freedom from sin whether the person would have a chance to get rebirth? Who wants to die? Who did good deeds in this life would they be deprived from getting rebirth since they would have nothing to suffer in their next birth? It is social recognition that our truthful deeds would pave the way for heavens. Our sinful deeds would take us to hell. Conceptions of heavens and hell are very strange though there does not exit any logical and scientific authentication. They are linked with religious faiths. Sometimes somebody comes down from heavens and should tell us about the truth there. Or else one reveals about the hardships of the hell.

Realist thinking considers that whatever the heavens or hell it is on this earth itself. Acts of human beings good or bad one has to have it on this earth only. It has been observed that people suffer when they find that they did commit wrong but it was too late then. When they reach to a point of no return by the time pain starts following him. Where the person so desires then by his good deeds he will make this earth heaven for himself in his life time. Or else by his bad deeds he would make his life hell. The man himself has created worldly pleasures or pains for himself. The man himself is the maker of his own destiny. He should not blame to his fore birth for his sufferings. He should not be disappointed by the deeds of his fore birth. Realism further goes to establish the very fact that there is nothing like fore birth or rebirth. How long the person will live under such unseen and unverified confusions? He should remember that he has got one life only and he would achieve nirvana during this life time only. One can himself testify this truth that nothing is left behind after the death. What is left behind is void. The human body constituted with earthly components finally meets with the earth.

This is an eternal truth that our life is full with pain. How good it would have been if we were able to make the scope of pleasure in the worldly pain itself? Why should there is pain in life? Simple reply because we are not able to liberate ourselves from badness. Our conduct is full with greed. We keep thinking about negative and hurting others. May be we do not gain but we remain worried about that the other should loose. We enjoy by causing loss to others. Possibly we fail to understand whether this kind of enjoyment carries with it the pleasure or the pain? In psychology it is termed as hedonistic pleasure. We forget this scientific truth that every action has an equal and opposite reaction. The opposite reaction of our hedonistic thoughts would already start in our mind meaning thereby that before we cause loss to others we started causing loss to ourselves. Mental injury is very dangerous. If it is due to opposite reaction then it would prove to be the root cause of all the pains to us. Your negativity of thoughts causes much harm to you comparatively and would keep disturbing you. One should then forget about attainment of nirvana during his life time that too when you yourselves are creator of all your pains. The concept of attainment of nirvana after death merely has the psychological angle. The person who was not able to make the scope of pleasure during his life time for himself then after death he would get nirvana it is not possible. The moments of pleasure of our life are the moments of nirvana that we lived life cheerfully and got to death with peace. The pain for ourselves we have created we can win over them provided we completely stopped thinking bad for others. This only would be the attainment of nirvana during our life time since no one has ever witnessed after death phase of human life.

"Once we are in the process of thinking bad resultantly we are bound to speak bad or do bad. You only can speculate within yourself about your deeds. When the nature has bestowed upon you the power of self-speculation then why do you fail in it? May be we are reckless and do not bother about our inner self. Make it a point then we are inviting sufferings for our own self. We just cannot escape from it. No one should be blamed for our self induced

sufferings. Achievement of complete nirvana during your life time goes with your attitude and the mindset. Attain nirvana by the strength of your mind. Never allow others to play with your mind. It reflects your mental weakness."

15

THE CLEAN MIND

Clean mind does not mean empty mind. Mind may be both full with good and healthy thoughts or it may be full with dirty thoughts, mind full with knowledge or lack of knowledge. If we happen to compare clean mind with any clean space then it denotes to an orderly image with full harmony and sanctity. Harmony everywhere facilitates and accelerates constructive activities because it provides serene atmosphere for the mind to develop ideas and thoughts. Creation is within domain of a healthy mind. A clean mind is bound to be a healthy mind for the reasons of its harmonious sanctity.

Relationship between the clean mind and spirituality about cleanliness in and around us is very significant. If our mind is getting polluted by dirty thoughts then it goes to prove that spiritual values are declining within us. If our mind is full with negativity then it is because of lack of spiritual orientation of mind. Do we need to define spiritualism? Spiritualism could be defined in a very simple manner as a kind of practice which makes one aware about his 'atman' i.e. his soul. It also develops awareness about 'antar atman' i.e. his inner soul. Spiritualism is a kind of human capacity to distinguish between what is good and what is bad. Once people are able to identify as to what is 'good' for others they start practicing about doing 'good' to others that is what is called spiritualism. Vices like greed, ego and anger are very individual among human beings. Once these vices start dominating over mind of the person they hamper the process of spiritual practice. Under the tight grip of these vices people fail to distinguish between the 'good' and the 'bad'. The pertinent question is that how to save our mind from the vices like greed, ego and anger? We always pray to the almighty to cleanse our mind and heart of all impurities. A clean mind is the space for ultimate spiritualism to set in and establish a direct interlink with 'godliness'. There are innate qualities of human soul like truth, peace, love, respect and purity of mind. Cleanliness of human soul directly connects with pure state of mind set which is essential for healthy human existence.

Clean environment plays a vital role in spiritual attainment of human beings. Similarly reciprocating to that spirituality pays it back in sustaining a clean and healthy environment. Spirituality has been often heard making a call that go to the nature, come close to nature and pay respect to it. Purity in our life has a direct bearing with mental balancing and harmony flavored with mutual respect not only among individuals but in complete consonance with the nature as well. We need to thoroughly observe that we identify our values with the nature we stay connected with the Almighty. Staying connected with the God helps to cleanse our heart and mind from all kinds of vices. This is the stage when we reach up to the spiritual attainment in our life. What is the relationship between cleanliness around us and the spiritualism? There is every possibility that our mind remained clean but the atmosphere around was dirty. Due to that dirty atmosphere there was more possibility of our mind getting polluted. Like that we did associate with such people whose mind was already not clean. We remained sharing our view with them. Our mental thinking continued to be influenced by their thoughts. Negativity leaves behind its imprints very fast in the mind of persons. Spiritualism has a direct relationship with the peaceful mental state of a person. Mind has strange capacity to search peace anywhere and everywhere. There should be no feeling as to searching peace of mind roaming through mountains and forests. Who would guarantee that one would attain peace of mind by sitting in mountains and forests? However, it would be dependent upon the firm determination of the person as to what extent he would be able to keep his mind clean? He remains untouched even while living amidst people with polluted thinking. It does not make any difference that whether he is in worldly life or away from it.

When it should be understood that a person has been charged with spiritual values? There was a change of thought in the person. He appeared to be completely transformed. It was noticed that now he did not think bad for others nor he did bad to others. Earlier he did not care about the social values. Violating social and personal norms used to be an easy task for him. His personal behavior was much critical and objectionable to others. He dared to cause harm to others and commit breach of peace. Now change of behavior was being witnessed which spoke volumes about his all round transformation. Whether this happened all of a sudden? He had started living very calm and cool. He became so sensible that nobody was hurt by him. He used to be perturbed now looking to the distress of others. If he was able to help them he helped them even beyond his capacity. He experienced divine pleasure out of all that since he had become spiritually charged. He started realizing that his life on this earth seems to be worth now. That was the life objective he could understand. What could be more than a person would need about the life spirituality and his clean mind? His life should be fruitful on this earth and nothing more. Meaning thereby that attaining a state of mind by means of wining over the impurities an individual could keep his mind clean all the way all the time. May be breaking away the social norms was an easy task for him but the kind of change in his behavior being noticed was in the direction of cleanliness keeping for away from impurities and was taking towards complete spiritualism.

We should not sit considering that it could have been possible overnight. The things are not that easy the way they appear to be but are not impossible either. It would be a rigorous process. We would have to pass through a phase of self-discipline which in itself is very strict. Association with careless people would not allow us to be disciplined. Lack of self discipline instigates us to commit such behaviors which are unfair and are not in accordance with our dignity. The person would feel momentary pleasure but that would not be positive. Impurities would get an entry into the mind and would stay there. If the person still goes careless then no sooner the impurities make a permanent place in his mind. Such unclean mind should leave any hope now to be spiritual.

When impurities are permitted to enter into the mind by the person himself then he is going to be liable for it. The mechanism of the human mind is such that whichever impurity it so feels it would throw it out. It would not allow the impurities to set in permanently. If impurities get a chance to stay then such minds are weak minds and could not be said to be clean minds. Once impurities are permanently set in the mind then one can easily imagine about the behavioral patterns of such minds. What could be then psychological condition of such person and of the people around him? Not only the immediate interests of humanity would be affected but future interests would also be damaged a lot if the human minds go so unclean. Alright…!!! It is understood that almost daily there are opportunities of such social contacts getting the minds unclean. There are very difficult possibilities to avoid such contacts but your mental strength lies in the fact that you remained untouched by these impurities. This in fact is your spiritualism in true sense that impurities around you could not adversely affect you. You remained absolutely clean and calm only by virtue of your mental strength. You become in such a position that even if few impurities happen to enter the mind you will either throw them out or they are not able to affect your mind any more. Make it sure that cleanliness of your mind as a rule must be the continuous process. Resultantly spiritualism would be the final end product of such continuous process. Continuity of any process in human behaviors could be rigorous but not impossible. Therefore, what we could learn is that a mind free from impurities is the first condition of spiritualism. Make a point for you to see that the impurities did not enter your mind. You can do it with the help of regular practice. You can be spiritualistic even while living in worldly life. Make yourself pure and clean at the same mentally tough and reasonable.

"Relationship between the clean mind and spirituality about the cleanliness in and around us is very significant. If our mind is getting polluted by dirty thoughts then it goes to prove that spiritual values are declining within us. If our mind is full with negativity then it is because of lack of spiritual orientation of mind. Do we need to define spiritualism? Spiritualism could be defined in a very simple manner as a kind of practice which makes one aware about his 'atman' i.e. his soul. It also develops awareness about his 'antar atman' i.e. his inner soul. Spiritualism is a kind of human capacity to distinguish between what is good and what bad."

———————————————

16

TRANSFORM ENERGY - CAN YOU?

Longing peace and containment of joy is the most important form of energy in your life. Being peaceful and joyful for you and for others as well would transform the entire world. There should not be any doubt about it. A person getting in anger frequently is very common. Why does one get angry? I am sure that you will feel realize that while you remain angry or even thereafter, you lose your peace of mind and the joy not only of yourself but also of the people around you. Anger is the negative energy which burns you from within. For the reasons of this burning only that your logical capacity inside you gets destroyed and you fail to take any proper decision. A person who is angry loses the balance of his thinking mind. If you are not able to properly think then you are also not supposed to properly act upon. If you fail to properly act upon then who is the looser? You only and none else…!!! People are seen going mad out of anger. Getting mad is the extreme impact of the negative energy being released of the anger. Who wants to go mad? Do You? No… not.

Why not to transform your negative energy into the positive energy of joy? You will notice that on occasions you make an attitude. You create your own self-image. One fine morning you find that you have completely become a prisoner of your own attitude and the self-image. You desire that the things should happen exactly the way you want.

This is your attitude. It is possible that the things do not happen that way. You become angry and lose your temper badly. That is how people get angry since they have become prisoners of their own attitude. They need to come out of it, if they really wish to get rid of anger and make their life happy with joy. You can justify your anger when you are acting in your administrative capacity. No doubt, this could be need of assignment you are performing. But always remember you are gradually developing a kind of attitude for yourself which is going to be your habit in due course. This in fact would not be fair.

Why do you become angry with others? Did you ever think about it? It is because the other person does not fit into the image you have made. How can you expect a person to be exactly up to the image you have made? It is the most pertinent question which anybody can ask. This is the mistake what most of us do. This is our problem and not the problem of the other person. You need to develop a kind of psychological mechanism within yourself that whenever you feel to practice your attitude as per the existing situations you do it. At the same time you should be in a position to immediately come out of your self-image by dropping your attitude and bringing yourself to the level as the situation so demands. Keep remaining within your self-image is dangerous. Emotions have convertible energy. Your attitudinal emotions can be transformed into joyful energy provided you apply it wisely to dilute such emotions to the extent that you come out of your self-prison. This is important for you to understand that continuing to be in anger for durations could be much harmful to you. Let us not lose our joy for petty anger.

We should not forget one thing that to overcome the emotions which make us angry is a very easy task. If attitudinal emotions are your problems then the solutions for the problem too lie with you only. Since the anger makes you blind from within you are not able to search for the solutions. Your open eyes means awakening with your inner consciousness. Why do you have any self-image? Your joyful personality would itself speak volumes about your image to others. Getting angry and being strict are the two different things. You could be strict without getting angry. Being strict reflects your principled image at the same time with no trace of anger. Where there is no anger the joy shall come to stay automatically without any extra effort of any kind.

There are varieties of social situations. People around you could be different in different perspectives. You need to be always prepared for a situation when people intentionally provoke you to become angry. They may be interested in disturbing your peace of mind. Your disturbed peace of mind would be a kind of sadistic pleasure for them. They would be jealous about the way of your life, your peace of mind and progress. They look for every opportunity or even create opportunities to put you in such a situation that your entire work plan is disrupted. The people with negative orientation around you are clever to the extent that they would be provoking you without getting themselves disturbed. They are so thick skinned that it hardly makes any difference for them for all that rubbish they would be doing around. And the problem with you is that you are sensitive enough and trapped by them very easily. Being sensitive is not bad but being too sensitive is also not fair, as it amounts to be weakness. Your sensitivity makes you alert and responsible. It is your sensitivity only which makes you mentally prepared to accept challenges in your life and you become ready to be made accountable. No problem.

But the problem starts here, when they succeed in getting you provoked since they never liked that you be a successful man in your life. They would be after you and would like to see you a big failure. True, it is the chemistry of human mind that the moment it is provoked, specifically when it is known to be sensitive, it loses its balance at the spur of the moment. You start getting angry over the man. That's exactly what that man wanted. He knows that now you would remain disturbed for a considerable duration, while at the same time he would remains absolutely untouched by the act what he did. You need to win over your weakness by means of transforming your energy, which not only you know but he also knew about it. That was the reason that he was able to put you down. The kind of energy whether negative or positive it works. When your mind is content with peace positive energy flows throughout your body and you are full with joy. It needs a rigorous practice for many years altogether to be content with peace of mind. You practice and you do.

Equally powerful is the negative energy which has been generated out of the anger. It starts burning you from within. The anger was not self- induced but it was the result of provocation by other. Self-induced anger is comparatively less damaging then the provoked one. Anger which comes from within you is due to lack of your content mind. Provoked kind of anger is more damaging for the reasons because you link that with your attitude and your self-image. Be aware of it as the people around you are out to damage you. Now, you would need the mental strength to convert and transform all that negative energy of anger into the positive energy. Yes…!!! You can do it. But off course, it is not an overnight job. Unarguably, every person looks for in search of peace of mind and joy. Please come out of your self-image. The man provoking you is to your self-image. Self-image being your own creation gets hurt very easily. Practicing transforming negative energy into positive one is no doubt a difficult process but not impossible. For all that transformation you only need an alert and conscious mind on day to day basis which keeps itself ready to counter all that provocation from the outer world. After a long continuous alertness you would find one day that you are completely transformed and nobody succeeds in provoking you. Your mind and body develops a kind of resistant power against anger. Transform this energy. Yes…!!! You can.

"Why not to transform your negative energy into the positive energy of joy? You will notice that on occasions you make an attitude. You create your own self-image. One fine morning you find that you have completely become a prisoner of your own attitude and the self-image. You desire that the things should happen exactly the way you wanted. This is your attitude. It is possible that the things do not happen that way. You become angry and lose your temper badly. That is how the people get angry since they have become prisoners of their own attitude. They need to come out of it, if they really wish to get rid of anger and make their life happy with joy."

17

TO BE SELF AWARE

To be aware of oneself is very significant in the sense to know who you are. Life management is nothing but understanding the life and live it up to the maximum of its happiness. What you demand from life? Or put it in another way, what the life demands from you? Why should the life demand from you anything after all? Before demanding anything from your life, the question which is quite pertinent is that whether what you have given to your life? Only keep on demanding from life. That's it. Getting aware to understand life is a continuous process. You need to meditate yourself for the purpose of developing this kind of understanding. To be self aware would be to be good, think good and do well for others. Ask yourself, whether you know the purpose that you took birth on this earth? Whether you lived up to the expectations of your life? If you think that you are self aware, it amounts to that you know yourself. Having to know yourself does not mean that you have developed the level of understanding as well. For many it takes the life time altogether but they still fail to understand about. They remained completely unaware and passed away. This was not the life meant for.

Being self aware is an essential component of human understanding. Who are you? You are a human being much superior to other living beings on this earth. You have to prove your existence better than the animals. On various occasions we fight each other worst than animals.

You may be practicing any religion of your choice but as a human being we are all one. May be you do not practice any religion but still you are the same human being but with a varied approach towards life. It matters the way you see your life and the life of other individuals. How do you feel that your life could be different than others? Religions are the codes of conduct for managing your life. No religion teaches for an extreme behavior against any one. All fellow human beings are equal irrespective of their religious beliefs. When the Almighty makes them to be equal then why the kind of feeling of hatred and discrimination we come across? What the life expected from you? You be kind enough with the other fellow human being. Could we do that? Was it due to lack of proper awareness? No, it was due to political hatred spread around by the power mongers. History reveals that they wanted to prove themselves to be super human beings. It is in fact personal thinking of a man if he goes for love to another human being or he hates him. Where you hate another human being it is not going to be your human feel. Where you risk for your human feel then you are not self aware and a lesser human being.

Demanding from life could be seen in different perspectives, like developing the capacity to demand from yourself and also the understanding as to the demand. By practicing through meditation people are able to control their attention on demands. Being focused and attentive enhances your capacity to demand. At the same time it also enhances the capacity of your own self to quickly respond to your demands. Both the situations of demanding and responding are complimentary and interdependent to each other. You demand from yourself that you need to have a focused mind for all the time. See that you have already prepared yourself to fulfill the demand. Your life provides a support system to you so as to ensure that your body and mind strongly respond to your demands. Demanding from your life must be seen as you are doing that as a matter of right. Life would also feel obliged to while considering to your demands related to your life management. You could make yourself capable to at least demand rightfully. The life would also feel good about it. In today's hectic and fast running world it is not that easy to control attention on self-awareness. The prevailing environment around is full of struggles in day to day life of an individual which fails to encourage self-awareness. It could be easy for a man to go to hills and practice meditation there to be self-aware, because he would get the environment and the peace of mind which would enable him to concentrate much easily and for a longer duration. The advantage being in such an environment is that it would encourage self-awareness. Thorough researches in the areas of meditation reveal that life can only be lived in present. This is an essential fact in our life which we need to understand seriously. People either living in past or living in future. How does it is going to help them? Alright...!!! One can argue that it is very difficult to forget the past. It has been the past of one's life which a person has already lived in. His experiences of past life are closely linked with it. It could be like this too. Past experiences on occasions are inspiring also. But such experiences can only be utilized as inspiration unless we are attentive enough to carry on with them. Otherwise it would go waste. It goes without saying that while living in present with controlled attention we would be in a position to get advantage from our past experiences. That would in fact mean to be self-aware when we are able to learn from our past. Whether it happened to be good or bad, if it was bad then learn to not to repeat that in present. While it was good then learn to add more goodness to it by multiplying it more nicely.

Past has already gone. Future is yet to arrive at. Past we have already lived, whether good or bad. Future we presume to be good definitely by making honest and sincere efforts by living in present. No doubt about it that by doing well in present we would be able to shape a better future. Thus the conclusion going to be is that by all means living in present is significant. Living in past or future is practically not possible. It is only in imaginations. A person can remember and imagine life in his past and the future. One can remember those events already happened in past and his imaginations could be based upon his future perceptions. Now living back in past would not be possible. We would make efforts to be self-aware by remembering the past and while living in the present. Keeping one self-aware within the society and maintaining social obligations simultaneously is difficult. A man with family and social obligations has to perform his daily pursuits, offer praying, to attend to religious rituals, at the same time maintaining a kind of balance with the problematic categories of people he comes across in his daily life, people with negative orientations, overcoming traffic congestions up and down, clutters of his desk at the office and to keep his higher self alive at the same time. Throughout the day he may not be able to find time to think about his own self but still he practice to be self-aware merely if with his controlled attention he decides as to what to do rightfully or what not to do? Where a man's bonafide is clear, he is self aware.

Compare to the monk in the hills who gets soothing environment, practices through breathing and perceives through his senses. He perceives the presence of his life around him. He could see it, smell it about and sense it. Free from any kind of social obligations the monk gets a better and easier opportunity to be self-aware. The worldly man can also do the same. The need is that he should proceed with a mindset that he is aware of himself. He knows about what he is doing? What he is doing is right and would not hurt any other individual? His family and social obligations are way of his life. He is fully content about them. He does not have uncontrolled desires. He remains prompt in fulfilling his social obligations. He is equally self-aware to that of the monk who is practicing on the top of a hill.

Taking birth, living and reaching to the stage of death all takes place in present. We lived up to our satisfaction or not we knew better. Our satisfaction lies in the fact that we were self-aware about what we did. Remembering our birth and the memories we lived are the subject matter of our present but lie in the past. We are celebrating our birth in present and try to live it up to that past. By the morning we get up and till in the night we go to our bed our mind should look for the question every moment as to 'who I am?' Where I am now? And, what I am up to? We would keep getting reply to these questions automatically. Our mind would be full of sensibility that I am aware of myself with greater vision of perspectives towards my life and also towards the life of others. You should be in a position to say that now I am able to know myself and would make my sincere efforts to make others aware too.

"Past has already gone. Future is yet to arrive at. Past we have already lived, whether good or bad. Future we presume to be good definitely by making honest and sincere efforts by living in present. No doubt about it that by doing well in present we would be able to shape a better future. Thus the conclusion going to be is that by all means living in present is significant. Living in past or future is practically not possible. It is only in imaginations."

18

UNDERSTANDING RELATIONSHIPS

Do we need to discover a new society? Why this question arises after all? Whether the existing society is failing to deliver the goods in a proper manner? Establishment of world peace is important. If the existing society has been unable to inculcate a kind of sensibility among the generations towards a sustainable world peace then it is going to be a most dangerous situation for our future society. Who are guilty of such dangerous situations? Is it because of lack of proper understanding among the people? Who needs to understand whom? In my opinion a person needs to understand himself first. Understanding oneself is very easy but it requires a rigorous process to follow with. The question would be whether we are ready to follow the rigorous process? It definitely needs a mental preparedness.

Understanding oneself and understanding relationships among the people is an essential component for a sustainable world peace, order and sense of security. Understanding involves exploring the whole process of thoughts, to be prepared to respect mutual feelings and an honest determination to work upon it. If one starts using relationships without properly understanding himself then confusions are bound to prevail only to lead towards a misunderstanding of him and others. Why do we fail to realize this very fact that this world is nothing but a display of lovely relationships among its people? An orderly world is not possible without understanding and respecting mutual relationships. If one is not able to properly understand himself how could he be in a position to claim for understanding others? This in fact is the virtual dilemma as an impediment for finally attaining the world peace. We fail to make peace.

Looking to today's perspectives we need to have revolution across the globe for the purpose of establishing world peace. Revolutions should not be misunderstood with a mass movement. There appears to be no necessity of mass movement for any revolution to go through. Revolutions are quite silent and primarily individual. When you understand yourself, you understand others. This understanding generates love and affection among individuals and affords an opportunity for inwards evaluation of such relationships. Once on this earth we are in a position to strengthen the bonds of relationships between two people the world peace is bound to prevail. What we are supposed to do is the right action and which is possible only when we are able to properly understand and establish relationships amongst the people of this world. Let us make move forward and have a call for understanding relationship without doubt this earth is going to be heaven for us.

A very innocent question comes to my mind. After all what could be that reason as to we are not able to understand ourselves? Is it due to the fact that we did not make any sincere effort in that direction? Even if some efforts would have been made then this would have left behind as mere formality only. Do we consider it that we failed in understanding the things? As the formalities could not be able to stand on the grounds to realities? The reality of today's world is that lack of brotherhood among the people is clearly visible on this earth. The man is seen just running and running for an endless race. He could never know as to whom he intends to leave behind? Nations too are mutually competing with each other just to leave behind some of them and move ahead of others. The man is not able to think even when this run would turn violent? Violence is always red and blind. In violence there is clearly visible a kind of lunacy. The makers of violence go fanatic. What would be the level of understanding in a lunatic state of mind? There is no need to say anything about it. Whoever declares more number of people killed in the violence he considers that he is far ahead of others and is the winner. The other one in his comparison could kill lesser number of people only so he is the looser and has been left much behind. They claimed victory but ultimately humanity was defeated. Battles were fought and won but nation's boundaries were left much tense. A number of people killed another number of people. Nations remained full with revenge. They remained enemies not for decades but for centuries. Looking to their tense relationships it appears that they would continue to be enemies in coming years too. They have not left any scope behind for mutual understanding and developing of relations. Whether humanity is above nations or nations are above the humanity? These things are so battered with each other that the nations have no time spare to sit together and think for some way out. They could have looked for some situation to establish mutually amicable relationships. Who is the winner or who is the looser? Is there somebody? Who could reply to my question? I know it is not that easy for anyone.

We are always ready to understand other persons but are least interested to understand self. Is it that our ego comes in between? Making no efforts to understand self but keep making declarations about having understood others. That's not the way? You cannot clap single handedly. Impossible..!!! By this way then world peace cannot be established on this earth. Please do not make statements that we have developed the kind of understanding of relations and that we would be able to establish world peace one day. It would be just day dreaming. Dreaming is a good but it would need to be worked upon. Understanding of relationships is not at the level of individuals only. It has its own strategic global parameters too. There are treaties prepared and signed between nations for the purpose of removing mutual tension. People are made to believe that these would be implemented. Before our expectations convert into belief the treaties are broken down. Serious violations are done even by the nations which are signatory to it. Now not only mutual tension increases but our relations become bitter than earlier. After all who had to pay the price of this mutual bitterness among nations? Who became the victim of it? Who lost his life? Who killed whom? Undoubtedly...!!!

The innocent people of the nations are the real sufferers of such bitterness. They never desired that there would have been bitterness among them. They never had either. What they desired was simply the peace and tranquility on this earth. There should have been understanding or relations which is strong foundation of such relations. No one should be blood thirsty of another human being. There should be human and their humanity.

Our understanding of mutual relations has been spoiled. We cannot deny from this fact. Our entire humanity becomes victim of individual fanaticism of a few. May be our leadership is adamant to understand it but it is dangerous that people of nations too keeping silent about it. People need to break their silence, for this they do not need any permission from anybody. World leadership is expected to perceive that this could happen when they would not be able to stop people from marching ahead. People of the world are silent this should not be interpreted that they cannot speak. People's silence is indicative of their patience and the faith they depose in the world leadership. They trust that understanding of relations among nations would be stronger and would persist. They would not tolerate if they feel betrayed by the world leaders. People know that they would initiate it by strengthening their personal relations. They are aware of this fact that a person need to understand himself first. They have expectations from the nations that they too understand themselves first. Initiatives would have not only to be made honestly but they should also appear to be made. We need to avoid this thinking that the other one should come forward with the initiative first. Where the ego comes in between then straining in relations will continue to be there. It is always advisable that there should be no scope of clash of ego among individuals then you will witness the understanding of relations and their foundations getting stronger. We would do it for the sake of humanity and its further betterment and also with a view to establish world peace.

"Why do we fail to realize this very fact that this world is nothing but a display of lovely relationships among its people? An orderly world is not possible without understanding and respecting mutual

relationships. If one is not able to properly understand himself how could he be in a position to claim for understanding others? This in fact is the virtual dilemma as an impediment for finally attaining the world peace. We fail to make peace."

19

BROKEN HEARTED AT PEACE

Search in peace for those who are with broken heart. Let us not go for the reasons behind broken hearted. There could be variety of reasons behind. It's as simple as that love, business, war, politics and the like. Go sure unless you are with a broken heart, you are falling short of perfection in your life. Parker Palmer has written an essay on, "The Politics of the Broken-Hearted." He writes very interestingly that 'There is no way to be human without having one's heartbroken'. The real challenge for the life follows as to how to live with the broken heart? How to maintain a balance between the peace of mind and the broken heart? Heart and mind are centers of emotional balance in human body. It makes a difference for the people who are sensitive and the people with thick skinned as well.

People carry on with the wounded heart for a long time. It is harmful for physical and mental health of the person and of other people too. The only option available is either to live with your heavy heart and ruin this beautiful life or to ease the heart out for a resolution with an open heart and become free from all pain. It would not be advisable to seek revenge for the broken heart. To seek to hurt the one who has hurt us. It would be an unending process to cause injury in retaliation of the broken heart surely at the cost of peace of mind.

Let us try to understand it other way round. Broken hearts are the open hearts. There is a famous saying that, 'God breaks the heart again and again and again until it stays open.' What a great thought particularly when you intend to buy peace for the mind. If we are ready to accept any adverse situation with an open heart it would make a miracle of joy and happiness in our life. Palmer explains further, "Imagine that small, clenched fist of a heart 'broken open' into largeness of life, into greater capacity to hold one's own and the world's pain and joy." Thus a broken heart remains an open heart. Let us feel this truth in this manner and resolve to the greater goal of a better life for everyone. An open heart is ready to accept the things the way they are in a most positive way and creates a room within for peace not only for itself but for humanity at large. It is for us only to resolve whether to have our hearts loaded broken or broken open. Our mind will rest in peace then and also mental peace to everyone.

There could be many reasons for broken hearts. These reasons are self created by the person himself. Reasons of love, like either you fell in love or your heart went out of your control and started chasing the one it liked. Proverbs were made like you have no control on your heart. If your falling in love has been one sided then your heart was to be broken one day, that was sure. It was in fact surprising that how could not you sense it earlier? By the time you could control, your heart had been already hurt. Now you are searching for the reasons that who was responsible? Now what for searching around? Now to whom you are blaming for? You would not be able to get the reasons. At the same time you would keep holding your hurt broken heart. Would not you like to be alright from this pain? Obviously...!!! You would like to be perfectly alright. Then who stops you? Never think that your broken heart was scattered around. Think this way that the knots of your heart are untied. Now you heart has been opened. It's nice that your heart has been unloaded and has become free from all burdens. Where you happen to bear loss in your business, it could be a reason for your broken heart. But it does not mean that you would sit around tired with defeat. This way you will become sick. It was not the objective of your life. This will not do. This is not going to instill peace in the broken heart. If you keep sitting with broken heart then forget about the peace returning back to normal. This you would need to examine as to where you did commit the mistake and you lost in business? You would have to ensure that such mistake is not repeated. There would be no mistake and you will progress in your business. Why would then there be any reason for a broken heart? This precaution you should have taken right from the beginning. Doing business means it should run and that should be the determination.

You are not getting the job you are looking for. It does not mean that you are not making efforts or struggling for it. But it happens that despite sincere efforts you fail to get through. You are shocked with blind eyes. You feel that nothing is acceptable to you less than your aim. You are now broken hearted as if everything has been lost in your life. You become loaded with the feeling that now what is the meaning of such life? This is a dangerous thought. This is not fair. You need to avoid such negativity at any cost. It is no way out. Never forget that your life is invaluable and full of infinite possibilities. There are unlimited possibilities for you. But for converting those possibilities into reality you only would have to make efforts. Making efforts only would not do. The condition would be that you need to make honest and sincere efforts. Believe it that the success would touch your feet. No force ever in this world can stop you from moving forward in your life. It may not be necessary that immediately after performing your honest efforts you are going to get your desired success. It is possible that the success may be delayed. Now you need to keep patient. Such moments only are the testing moments of your life. Remember that no examination of your life would be exactly the way you like it. Success in the examination would depend upon the level of your preparation. Delay in getting your success should not be the reason for your broken heart. Here comes a new thought before you. Your broken heart means opening up of your heart, a freedom from lying hurt post broken hearted.

There is a big percentage of success for an open heart instead of broken hurt one. Now when your heart is open after it was broken, its capacity to dare to challenges has been enhanced. Your thinking should be that after heart break it is not scattered but has now enlarged being opened up and has entered into the bigness of your life. Opening up provides you the peace of your broken heart around you only. You have trained your mind in this manner that the pain of the broken heart could not disturb you. This great thought of your mind would certainly take you to the great heights of your life. May be that the shape of your success is not the like you thought it, but it would be definitely be in its vastness which you never imagined. By continuously supporting your broken heart the Almighty prepares you for such challenges in your life. Now you become ready to enjoy the unlimited peace of your mind. You realize that the Almighty is great. That's it.

"People carry on with the wounded heart for a long time. It is harmful for physical and mental health of the person and of other people too. The only option available is either to live with your heavy heart and ruin this beautiful life or to ease the heart out for a resolution with an open heart and become free from all pain."

20

THE SERENE MOMENTS

Serene Moments…? Can you define serenity? Instead of defining serenity one can feel it by heart in a much better manner. There could be a question whether it is within our control to remain calm and peaceful? The reply would be in positive. Yes…..!!! It is possible. Anger is a very natural human reaction. Are the moments of anger are serene moments? Yes…!!! You can feel that. While you are angry you could never be peaceful. Worst is going to happen to you if you are allowing your anger to stay on and continue in your body and mind for a longer duration. It is very difficult to avoid people annoying you, making you angry. But you can buy serene moments for you by maturely controlling your emotions arising out of such anger and annoyance.

Forgiveness is the most significant mature emotion in humans which has wonderful capacity in not allowing the anger to creep in your heart and stay on. Resentment and unforgiveness induces one to hold on the anger in heart. Such holding on puts very dangerous impact on the immune system of human body and leads the person to a state of permanent stress. If you so make them, serene moments do possess spiritual touch. For sure there is an obvious connection of body, mind and soul when one claims to attain serene moments. This is possible to attain through perseverance and sustained practicing of forgiveness. Practicing forgiveness may appear to be a difficult task for a person for their emotional reasons but is not impossible at all. Sufficient researches have been conducted to understand links relating to working of the body with the thinking process of the mind. Serene minds are spoiled once the thinking process of the mind is disturbed. Our emotional disturbances are seen promptly reflecting in our body as a result of internal war we fight within ourselves. We could have overcome this in fight situation with the help of forgiveness. We could have saved our body and mind from any such acute emotional stress. Among human beings nervous breakdown could be the end result of all such reactionary processes. There could be situations you are going to face that people may start considering your forgiveness as your weakness. This could again be a typical situation for you to face with. But always make it a point that such situations are going to prove to be the real test of your emotional strength. Do not bother. When you always feel content within yourself even during adverse times than be sure you are strong. It would hardly make any difference for you that people think your forgiveness as your weakness. Forgive them since these moments would only be your virtual serene moments.

Please make it a point. In an adverse world like this it often becomes very difficult to remain serene. Then you need to buy serene moments for yourself at any cost. Take for instance the profession you are working in. You have number of professional adversities. If you happen to be sharp and professionally bright amongst people with negative mind set then you are inviting trouble for yourself. People in your profession are jealous of your talent. They are also not happy by your performance and progress in the profession. They would be looking for opportunities so that they can pull you down. There are possibilities that they become successful in damaging you for the reasons that you are left alone while they are in good numbers and united to harm you. This is the big tragedy of survival on this earth where you can face such kind of sharp negativity. They are successful to snatch away your serene moments. Instead of bothering for their own business the majority of them create problems for others. They look worried as to how one is living healthy and cheerful life? If you are single mindedly concentrating in your profession and obviously doing good work then be sure they will trouble you. You always need a peaceful mind to progress yourself. You can make it a point to be content within yourself. What to do then of the people who are out to disturb your serene mind? The moment they are able to snatch peace of your mind your concentration for your work is gone. That is what in fact they wanted. But you just do not bother. If they want to trouble you, that is their problem. Let them handle with their problems. You just keep performing and make your progress forwards.

It happens to be a good question as to what does it mean buying serene moments? Does it not amount to surrender before such elements in a bid to buy serene moments from them? It may amount to bowing down on the knees for a compromise. Would this not be taken by them as weakness of such person? Alright, this question is technical indeed. Make it a point first that you cannot buy anything from the persons who have nothing to sell. They are empty handed and they continue to be like that only. How could they be able to give you something when they themselves do not have anything? Forgiveness is unparallel of any human activity. It is an attitude which you need to inculcate within yourself. There is no need to surrender before anybody for the purpose of buying serene moments for you. Developing an attitude of forgiveness is a very rigorous process. It takes even a life time for a man to achieve this attitude but possibility is more that he would fail. You are fighting within yourself to attain this in totality. Once you are able to achieve this then only you would be in a position to realize the inner strength of forgiveness. It is agreed that you may be needed to bow down on your knees before your own inner self and not before such people. That is the struggle within you which goes on throughout your life since you are a sensitive man. Being sensitive is your strength. You become angry at the spur of a moment. It is not your fault but it is a human weakness. This would make you sick. The point is that you have to overcome this human weakness provided you wish to be a strong man. You are attaining a virtue for your inner strength. It should never be misunderstood as surrendering before anybody. The brightness of your attitude would reflect in your personality in such a manner that people of such nature would not be able to dare to stand before you.

Forget about that they would even be able to disturb you. No doubt, you would achieve this only through perseverance. Mind it, you will not allow losing your temper come, what may. This is again not an easy task. You would be bowing down before yourself, only to see that you are coming out of your self-image. Living in a self-image is dangerous. Forgiveness will help you to come out of it. You will feel what you enjoy? You are serene. Your mind would be full with peace. This is the way you are undergoing to buy serene moments for yourself. You are the ultimate winner make sure. No compromise.

"When you always feel content within yourself even during adverse times, than be sure that you are strong. It would hardly make any difference for you that people think your forgiveness as your weakness. Forgive them, since these moments would only be your virtual serene moments."

21

CARE FOR CHILDREN

Children are the very delicate mind. They need proper parental care in their childhood so that they can grow healthy physically as well as mentally. Attachment of the parents for their children is quite natural. Attachment is for their betterment, getting them strong and responsible youth. That's true. But it is often noticed that attachment makes people psychologically weak. Because of the weakness of psychological nature the children become victims of it. The situation being posed by this parental expression becomes quite difficult when one starts thinking in terms, as to what a parent should do while making his love and attachment for their children? At the same time without getting the child victim of such attachment. Researches reveal that too attachment not only makes the parents to become weak from within for their children but at the same time it also enhances the possibilities of their children to become a deviant one.

What makes a child getting deviant behavior? What the parents should take care in upbringing their children? It has been seen that many parents do not care about small things like they keep giving money and other facilities to their children without any justifiable reason. It is agreed that this may be out of mere love and attachment on part of their parents. But they forget that the child is developing a kind of bad habit in spending that money uselessly and craving for more luxurious life in future years. Why do not parents exercise control over indiscriminate expenditure habits of their children? Why the parents give this much money after all to their children which induces them to develop bad habits? What will happen when sensing the trouble mounting ahead, the parents stop giving money to their children all of a sudden? The child is bound to go aggressive against parents.

The virtual trouble for the parents lies ahead since the child has already gone deviant. Now at this stage to stop giving him money all of a sudden would make him aggressive. He would go rebel against the parents without realizing this fact that what they are doing is for his benefit. Parents need to realize the situation which has arrived at. Primarily the parents are to be blamed for all that which has happened or is likely to happen with his child in the years to come. It is noticed that the parents getting more possessive towards their children is also harmful to them in long run. Being possessive in the sense that not letting the children to be the architects of their own destiny. With a supportive and vigilant control over children we the parents can make our children to be best decision makers in future life for their better performance and achievements. The supportive vigilance in the child needs to be inculcated by the parent right from their childhood. We can save our children for sure from any delinquent behavior. It will not only ensure a joyful future life for themselves but for the parents too. No doubt, love and care is for the parents to their children but it should never be at the cost of the child getting rebel or vegetative. The care and attachment from the side of the parents must be flavored with intellectual vigilance towards the future of the child.

There are situations in our world civilizations where communities worry about their children so that they can keep them away from luxurious life. Conveniences appear to be good in favorable conditions only. The time would always remain favorable, who will take this guarantee? Our elders say by experience that the time always does not remain the same. When time is going good one should enjoy it fully. While in the times of adversities child is made to be mentally prepared so that the adverse situations do not break him out. Whether we have trained our children to be ready for such situations? We need to make our children psychologically strong that they have to move ahead in their life. They should not be made slaves of comforts but made to struggle so that success touches their feet. They are able to make their own conveniences once they suffer through and develop their will power strong. If there are adversities in their life they need not to be worried at all. If there happens to be something adverse still there is no need to be worried about. We need to tell our children this very fact that where there is no trouble in life and if they are not able to defeat that by facing it then their life goes waste. Troubles in their life make them stronger. They only face troubles in their life who take risks head on. If we parents are not making our children taking risk then we are making them trouble shy in their life. Once the children are not scared of risks then troubles would not deter them and success would become their habit.

Whatever, the children achieved in life by making struggle that only is going to be permanent for them. The parents need to understand that this being the real enjoyment of life for their children. What they get without making struggle would be temporary in nature, disturb them and would not let them to enjoy their life. Such failures could discourage our children. They would be broken at heart and not be able to progress ahead. Momentary success was never the objective for our children. We should not forget that children are the future of any society. In any era the necessary condition for a strong society is that as to how seriously and honestly we have invested good thoughts among our children? In true sense the worry for the character and mental strength of our children must be the global concern. It is for the society also to think upon it for the task to be done so that the future of the society gets a better direction. It is our liability too. It must be a collective responsibility of every one of us not only being strict but simultaneously an absolute one. In case the child happens to deviate from the rightful path and proceeds to wrongful way then the child is not to be blamed. All the blame would be that society failed to give its children the rightful lesson so as to make them move with a positive set of mind. It should be for that nation too, to be worried about its children. A nation could never develop by neglecting its children. Parents could care him only till he was at home. Education system is the back bone of nation building. We cannot escape from providing them better education. Let the education system ensure that every child goes to schools. Let the nations now think about it. We do not need a society which keeps shedding crocodile tears instead of doing something for its children. The children are the capital of our nation. It must be our concern as to how to manage this capital? Otherwise we would be a broken scattered weak society.

"It is noticed that the parents getting more possessive towards their children is also harmful to them in long run. Being possessive in the sense that not letting the children to be architects of their own destiny. With a supportive and vigilant control over children we the parents can make our children to be best decision makers in future life for their better performance and achievement."

————————————————

22

LAW OF ACTION

Law of action is complex in the sense that when we perform action, we are told that you should not desire for the fruits of your action. For we people, as the persons of ordinary prudence, it looks like completely impractical to do action without a dream in our mind. We find it very difficult to completely disassociate ourselves from the desire to have a result for our action. Law of action demands disassociation from such desire. If we are not able to dissociate ourselves from desires of fruits then it becomes very difficult to keep a balance with this law of action. What is wrong if we desire results of our action? Are we not going to be disappointed if we lose despite we put in untiring honest and sincere efforts? We need to understand this philosophy of action in its true letters and spirit. The philosophy speaks out that you have a duty only to perform an action and not a right to its fruit. Meaning thereby that it speaks more for a person to be duty bound rather than claim for any right for desired results. Undoubtedly we perform a good deed to the best of our honest efforts with some conscious or unconscious desire for a good result. Where do we stand wrong if we so desire? If we help somebody then we have a hidden desire in our mind that this help will satisfy his needs. We do 'invest' our deeds in present through our action so that we may enjoy its 'dividends' in future.

We should work with an optimistic mindset that if we are doing well then its results will also be good. Why not...??? Yes...!!! I do agree with this argument that we perform our action satisfactorily good but still we do not get desired results. This infuses a kind of disappointment and ultimate frustration and our orientation starts becoming negative. We need to stop this situation to happen since this frustration is going to harm us only. We did the best what was within our reasonable limits and efforts to be performed. At the same time we should make it a point that it is not essential that our efforts should get exactly the same results the way we wanted. Doing our actions perfectly is within our control but getting results the way we want could not be within our control. Still there always remains a ray of hope if we are not disappointed and continue to perform our action effortlessly. We should not forget that our effort never go waste. It brings more perfection with the passage of time. The results you get much time better than you ever expected. Destiny always intends to make a person more perfect and perfect through rigorous performance of his deeds. Let us not forget that it is only the conscious or unconscious desire which perpetuates the law of action in its true letters and spirit making people reach their pinnacle of glory ultimately.

Laws of action may appear to be complex but that is not so. They are included in the general rules of our life management. Basic mantra of life success is the supremacy of action. We are bound to do action and that too keeping ourselves strictly within rules of action. Where a person considers that keeping oneself within rules is very difficult then laws of action are going to be complex. The question in our mind must be that can we survive without doing action? The very existence of human has been linked with it either doing good action or bad one. Good action is going to give you the peace of mind with the flow of happiness to your entire body. You feel within yourself the satisfaction of your action. Your bad action is definitely going to disturb you. You did that but it kept pinching to your mind that you should not have done it. If you remained so disturbed then this is not your achievement. You are the loser. You started repenting of what you did. Make sure, your mind would now come with determination to not to repeat bad action again. This is your achievement which you are going to enjoy. That only is the fruit of your action. Search for the peace of mind ends that too without much wandering around. Your mind content with peace is biggest goal of your successful life. Your practicing of rules of action made it possible.

We are human beings and having weaknesses within us are quite natural. Whatever the action we do, we link it with availability of fruits. This comes to our mind that we did action, now the fruits should follow. There should be nothing wrong in it. This is very simple. We did action so we desired for fruits of our action essentially. Actions bearing fruits or actions bearing fruits essentially, these could be two separate conclusions. One would die if he fails to perform actions. That is going to be the law of nature. Irrespective of the fact whether you desire for the fruits or not, it is going to yield fruits depending upon the kind of efforts you put in, flavored with integrity and purity of your action. Essence of your action is that fruits are going to follow. You did good action, certainly expect for good results. You did bad action then do not look for good results. You are going to be disappointed, it is certain. Bad actions would yield bad results only. The rule is that you cannot assess yourself about your actions. How could one give a certificate to himself that he is good? After all no one would like to give himself the certificate for bad. Surely he would not, the matter ends then. Even if you happen to give good certificate for you who cares? People are not going to accept that.

You would have experienced when you did good actions, you worked hard. But still you did not get good results. You failed. Obviously, you were disappointed. Anyone would be disappointed. You went in depression thinking that you did make all efforts as was expected to be done under the circumstances but it all went in vain. This is the psychology of human nature. When one does not get success in life despite good efforts then human mind gets hopeless. Again comes up the same question. Who are you to assess your action by going against the rules of nature? If you happen to assess yourself naturally you are going to assess yourself to be good. You should do that since you have put in hard labor, you know. Everybody does it. You cannot be an exception. Where the result was not up to your expectations, you will be disappointed. Suppose…!!! You did what you were not having within your scope to act. That way you have invited trouble for yourself to get disappointed. Do not blame any other person for this trouble. This only is the law of action. It is not complex. You made it complex for yourself.

While in search for a job you go to appear for the interview. You perform better in the interview that is your good action. But you are not supposed to assess your interview. Your interview would be evaluated by the subject experts who have interviewed you. You have to perform better that is only within your control. Your claim is there to get that job. But other candidates also have the similar claim and perform better since all the candidates possess the eligibility for that post. Then whether all the candidates would be declared successful in the interview? No…!!! You cannot take the decision that you should get that job. This decision would be taken by the expert interview board only. They would only after your assessment during interview would declare you either successful or not successful. If you are declared successful then you would be happy otherwise you would be disappointed. You thought that your interview was quite good. But this was your assessment. Rule says that assessment of the interview board would be final. So we would have to do our action and leave the desire of the fruit subject to the laws of action. After the results are declared, we are left with no other option except to admit this very fact that the candidate who was selected for the post by the interview board was surely better than others at the time of interview. Leaving behind doing your action by disappointing yourself is not going to help you in any manner. Keep doing your actions with sustained efforts this only is the life one lives in true spirits of life management. Law of action seemed to be complex to you when you were not successful by your assessments. Otherwise rules were not that complex. Ask from the candidate about it that was successful. He will surely welcome that he did action and got the fruits of success. Supremacy of action means sustained actions. No any other alternative. Doing your actions sincerely and honestly and getting success.

"We did action so we desired for the fruits of our action essentially. Actions bearing fruits or action bearing fruits essentially, these could be two separate conclusions. One would die if he fails to perform actions. That is going to be the law of nature. Irrespective of the fact whether you desire for the fruits or not, it is going to yield fruits depending upon the kind of efforts you put in, flavored with integrity and purity of your action. Essence of your action is that fruits are going to follow."

———————————————

23

ZERO-THE MIND

We count the numbers as 1, 2, 3, 4, 5.........then 9. What comes after number...9...? Number 9 is considered to be a complete number to its maximum. Rest is the combination of different numbers. What is the concept of zero? Where the zero stands? Zero also makes the combination of numbers but without any other number it is referred to as nothingness, emptiness or void. In India we do consider it as 'shunya'. Shunya is the whole sky which refers to a state of wholeness or fullness.

The state of zero minds is a complete spiritual mind which we all attempt to achieve. Now let us consider whether we can achieve this stage? Mind is a seat of thinking process. It may be a positive thinking process or a negative one. Zero minds do not mean absolute emptiness of thoughts. Void also denotes to equilibrium and we would attain the stage of equilibrium only when our thinking process has positive orientation. We cannot expect a human mind with a zero thought. That's in fact is the point of distinction of a human mind from an animal existence. We must honestly experience that we allow negative thoughts to creep in our mind. Negative thoughts are very dangerous to upset the mental equilibrium. Once the mental equilibrium is upset we cannot achieve a void or zero state of mind and here goes away the mental peace.

Meditation is the rigorous method to regulate the mental equilibrium through continuous generation of positive thoughts. One would need to attain the equilibrium and it must stay on in one's mind. That would only be a zero state in true sense, a void mind. A sense of void gives a feeling of having everything and completeness. In an embryo of the mother, life is generated out of complete zero state to its final fullness. In Buddhist philosophy it has been categorically defined that completeness is the absolute reality of life. Our all meditative efforts would fail unless we approach our life with zero set of mind to fill it up only with positivity. This is known as zero state of the mind.

As I have said right in the beginning of my discussion. Where 'zero' if seen from the viewpoint of arithmetic then it is of no value. But without zero too things would not materialize. To move forward the highest number …'9'… in its chain we need to take into account zero then only there would be joining of numbers to reach to its completeness. For understanding zero state in its true sense we would need to go through a complex spiritual process. My humble submission would be that if we would time and again talk about literal meaning of zero then it would look like void only, as if completely empty, meaning nothing. A big zero. This is correct that if we place zero before any number its value would not increase. But when the zero has been placed after any number then its value keeps increasing. If one zero is placed then the value of that number would increase tenfold, by two zero its value would increase hundred fold. Meaning thereby, it's not like that the zero has no value. Its value would be dependent upon its placement.

I wish to talk about void of the mind but I reached up to zero. The only purpose to understand was that zero be not seen merely in the sense to be zero. Possibly this zero state only controls the nature and our mind too. Sky is synonymous to zero. In case zero means nothing then sky also would mean nothing. How would we take the risk to consider the sky to be zero? Sky only is the destination ultimately. Means that we can reach up to the sky can balance and move around. Does zero state of mind mean empty mind? Can mind be void? Natural function of mind is thinking process. The mind would keep performing its function to think. One would have either good thoughts or bad.

Whatever is the nature of thoughts the mind would be full of it. Mind would be full with dirty thoughts, so you wish you can fill the mind with clean thoughts as well. It's your mind and the choice too would be yours only. Who would like to fill mind with dirty thoughts? Who would allow his body to be dirty? But still, dirty minds are there. These dirty minds spoil the entire social system. Who allows these minds to be filled with dirt? The people in society make their mind full with dirt. Where the individual makes a determination that he would not allow the bad thoughts to make entry into his mind then how could there be dirty minds? Impossible, we pose to keep away from badness but at the same time we keep roaming with dirty thoughts in our mind. This is our mutually contradictory double standard. This would not do and would make fall of the society a certainty. Nations would also come into the loop.

The beauty of zero minds lies in the fact that those minds with full of variety of thoughts but still they enjoy the pleasure of a void mind. Great spiritual thinkers are of the opinion that minds with full of thoughts could still be void. Attaining the zero state of mind is the final objective of human life. Whether you are able to achieve it or not this would be dependent upon the standard of your thoughts. You would be thinking that when there is a continuous flow of incoming and outgoing of thoughts in your mind, then what would be that stage when the mind would go zero? Yes...!!! That's the thing. That stage of a living mind when it enters into the state of zero thoughts. It stops thinking for moments a peaceful serene mind. This is the spiritual achievement. The great spiritual leaders achieved this stage of mind completely and ultimately reached to the final goal of human existence. You must be thinking that how come human life stops thinking? It is against the nature. Going against the nature would mean if the mind ceases to exist. What you think is correct. The mind cannot go against the nature but it can select at least for good thoughts or it has to think badly.

Zero minds would be that state where there would be continuous flow of thoughts but the minds would not feel to be burdened of it since it would be filled with all positive thoughts only. Positive energy of such thoughts would keep the mind calm and cool. The mind would feel of zero thoughts in it because the mind would have no burden despite fullness. You would remain happy with joy. You have witnessed oceans to be serene despite deep full with water unlimited. Sky full with air, continuous flow of it but still the sky is void, zero. Serenity of your mind would end the moment there is scarcity of positive thoughts in the mind and the negative thoughts have somehow managed to enter into it in quantities. Since both these categories of thoughts are just opposite in nature to each other they would not be able to maintain a balance and would conflict with each other inside the mind. They would create a state of disturbed conflict mind. Then there is no reason that you are going to feel a cool and zero mind. Your mind has unlimited power to think. Every day countless thoughts enter to your mind in the form of positive and negative thoughts. Negative thoughts by nature have dominating character over positive one. Either you train your mind in such a manner that negative thought are not able to enter to your mind or even if they happen to enter to your mind the united strength of your positive thoughts are able to thrash them away your mind. Balancing of mind is possible where the mind after rigorous practice for years develops a kind of internal mechanism which counters negativity of bad thoughts in favor of positive ones. Mind fights conflicts, develops to control them and makes a permanent balancing of overlapping thoughts in your mind. You are now peaceful with joy. You have attained the zero state of mind. Automatically with formatting of your mind now without any extra efforts positive thoughts would keep coming in your mind and keep going. Your mind would never feel any burden of flow of thoughts. Negative thoughts would then never dare to come close to you. You are now in the zero state of mind.

"Zero minds would be that state where there would be continuous flow of thoughts but the minds would not feel to be burdened of it since it would be filled with all positive thoughts only. Positive energy of such thoughts would keep the mind calm and cool. The mind would feel of zero thoughts in it because the mind would have

no burden despite fullness. You will remain happy with joy. You have witnessed oceans to be serene despite deep full with water unlimited. Sky full with air, continuous flow of it but still the sky is void, zero."

24

BALANCING CONFLICTS

Changing circumstances are very common in human life. Nature is ever changing, so is the human nature. Conflicts are subject to increasing desires of a man. But at the same time human desires are also quite natural. Therefore, the conclusion would be that conflicts are bound to happen in human life. The only point would be as to how to balance these conflicts so as to avoid unpleasant moments in human life and live with happiness. So we need to learn to balance any challenging situation. Human capacities are very vast. A person can reach on the top of glory provided he possesses the tendency to take risks and keep moving. A very natural question arises in my mind as to how can a person think of living without desires in his worldly life? This is practically not possible. But there is a point which a person needs to keep in his mind. Desires are not bad all the times. One should make his desires exactly up to his personal human capacity to get that desire fulfilled. Every person well understands his own physical and mental capacity to work upon his desires. Then why to think beyond one's capacity? That is right. A person can enhance his capacity to perform by subjecting himself to hard work and rigorous practice through perseverance. Yes…!!! That could be possible and you can achieve the unbelievable. Enhance your capacity by putting yourself up to the hard work and think big even beyond, to be great. Great people of all times were able to do that hard work. They faced challenging situations in their life pursuant to their life objectives. They learnt to balance the conflicts of challenges in life and went on working beyond their capacities and became great for the sake of advancement of humanity better and better.

Make it a point that you will come across circumstances in your life which may trouble you. You factually understand better if you can do something to change adverse circumstances. Then why to be worried about it? Let opposite circumstances come to you. Work full capacity and out do such circumstances which are troubling you. At the same time there could be another situation that you find yourself for a moment to be not able to do anything to change the circumstances. Then why to be worried about it at all? Mind it, researches have proved that psychologically things would not be going beyond your capacity to work. Either work hard to enhance your capacity or forget about it.

Try to think that desiring to get things done beyond your capacity is going to be a conflicting situation. We would not be able to balance that unless we work upon to enhance our capacity. You will become upset since things would not go according to your calculations. This would be all unnecessary since you have invited trouble for yourself. Now either work upon it meticulously or withdraw yourself. Balancing of your conflicts is very essential instead of carrying on with conflicts in your mind. It would be relevant to all situations. It is always better to avoid conflicts by keep them at balance rather than to be distressed about all that. Distress would be a state of mind where you desire to improve upon the conflicting situations by means of understanding them and then looking for means to act upon them. Obviously, it is possible sometimes that you are not able to find instant solutions to deal with. This you must understand is going to be harmful for you. Balancing amounts to where you think yourself to do something to improve situations in a better manner. That is always great. Proceed further with it. But at the same time there should be no reason to be distressed about it where despite making sincere efforts you could not change the things. If you keep worrying about it then balancing process of the conflicts would be destroyed. It would further hamper your workability to handle incoming situations in your life.

Researches and elders experiences reveal that every such conflict you are going to encounter in your life has a solution provided you have developed the needed capacity to identify the problem and resolve it. It would never be wise to keep worrying for something you cannot change. In a social system you come across a situation when you seek to intervene in other's conflicts with an obvious motive to help them out. Your intentions are quite helpful but there are possibilities that you fail in resolving the conflicts of your near and dear one's. You may feel that despite your sincere efforts you failed and could not change the situations. It happens but it should not deter you. Resolutions of conflicts are dependent upon mental preparedness of others too relating to their problems. They seem to be not prepared despite your seriousness. You should not at all feel worried about it since they do not look to be bothered about it.

This is just like a married couple who are in conflict with each other. They feel that their family life has reached to a point of no compromise. They move divorce petition before a family court with a request that they should be separated from their wedding life. The judge understands the gravity of the conflict and its future consequences. With a view to help them out to resolve their conflict the judge makes his sincere efforts to counsel them so that they are convinced to reconsider their decision to be divorced. The judge understands that any divorce amounts to breaking of a family system leading ultimately to a weak society. Despite repeated opportunities given to the couple by the judge they seem to be adamant to resolve their conflict. The judge finds himself to be quite helpless to help them out in resolving their problem. He failed in changing their mind. Finally with a very heavy heart the judge allows their petition and grants them divorce. The very pertinent question arises then why should the judge to be worried about it at all? He knows that he made his honest efforts under the given circumstances. The conflict had its own solutions too in the law books. But the judge finds himself to be helpless and to be not able to do anything to change the mind of the couple regards their best interests.

On the basis of working of the conflict resolution mechanism of human mind the conclusion is that most of the situations of human life could be changed may be some of them are not. This is also true that most of the human conflicts are their own creations. It goes to show that resolutions to such self created human conflicts are possible. You cannot blame any other person for the reasons where you allowed yourself to become disturbed by inviting unpleasant moments. Be sure the way you allowed yourself to be upset you know the solution as well to undo that. Thus there should be no reason to feel unhappy and become agitated about a situation which is your own creation. You are the only person who better understands your capacity to work out any conflicting situation because you are not in a position to say it is someone else who made you upset. In a world like this as we come across today where majority of people believe in pulling others legs. It is very common today that people at large have nothing to do by your problems. They would create conflicts for you, move away and keep watching you from a distance to derive sadistic pleasure by putting you in trouble. Develop your own capacity to stiffly deal with such categories of conflicts to be able to absolutely having no affect by dirty tricks of such people. Here you need to take extra care and make extra efforts to stubbornly undo what others did for you maliciously to disturb you and to make you upset. See…!!! Always keep this fact in your mind that you are the best person to know about the situation and where you understand that change is possible. You start working for the change without any delay. You also know better at the same time keeping in mind the resources you are in that the change is not possible then why to cry for it? Accept that without any hesitation and without worrying yourself further. You worked within the bounds of what is possible? That should be your satisfaction. You will find that you are able to successfully resolve the conflict and that too without disappointing yourself.

It would be my humble submission that natural way of conflict resolution starts with the individual himself. The advice we give to others is first applicable to ourselves. Never forget that you are the only best well wisher of yourself. Off course, your parents do for you what they consider to be best for you. You might have noticed that your expectations from others mostly disappoint you. It would depend as to what extent the other person takes interest or is serious about resolving your conflicts. You should not have any dependency upon others. You might have observed that under such circumstances that despite your well wishers are with you around but the first initiative in resolving or balancing your conflicts comes from the side of you only. Well if they are there by your side, good. They are most welcome since there mere presence would boost your confidence. Feeling of any kind of disappointment on your part must be avoided when you know that it is going to be lone battle for you in resolving your conflicts. No doubt the first step towards conflict resolution comes from your side and the last step too but at the same time the well wishers who are much concerned about you are great in the sense that they felt to spare from their valuable time for you to help you out in balancing your conflicts. This would be a psychological kind of support from them what you needed most in your testing times. You must feel much obliged about them. This should be our strategy in life management that we should not wait for others to point out our problems. It should be a self realization process which you need to develop within yourself. Your own internal mechanism would start identifying the conflicts within you and look for the instant solutions for you to resolve them. Some of your conflicts may take longer duration to be resolved. No problem. You need to handle them with a cool mind. The options lie within you only when you start encountering with your problems without being overwhelmed by them. That is your patience by cultivating inner qualities within yourself which made you to succeed in balancing your conflicts and move on with complete confidence. This made you feel that the life is quite beautiful to be managed with love and passion. You need to live it up to. That's great.

"Researches and elders experiences reveal that every such conflict you are going to encounter in your life has a solution provided you have developed the needed capacity to identify the problem and resolve it. It would never be wise to keep worrying for something you cannot change. If you keep worrying about it then balancing process of the conflicts would be destroyed. It would further hamper your workability to handle incoming situations in your life."

25

HUMAN HEALTHCARE

World has a tremendous potential for growth. India as a country is not far behind. For effective social and economic growth of any country, what is needed is that human empowerment must be ensured through investment in health. Since its independence India has travelled a long journey and has achieved an amazing growth in IT Sectors, industries and entrepreneurship. Many countries of the world which are either developing or under developed are struggling hard in maintaining balance between health care and human care. Investment in health for poor and rich is alike. The factor which troubles most is that investment in health care would not be a big issue for rich people because they can afford it but would definitely be a matter of serious concern for the poor.

Studies on international levels reveal that there is a strong connection between the prosperity of a nation and the human health. Raw materials for a strong and dynamic society are the mental capacity of human resource and its corresponding labor productivity. Fertility of the human capacity and labor productivity of its population has been directly dependent upon investment in human health. The big question always stuck to my mind about the aforesaid investment vis-à-vis economic soundness of the nation. How could it be possible for poor nations to invest in human health which keep struggling for bare survival of its countrymen? They merely survive by whatever the level of healthcare is available to them. It is not any secret that proper health care has become a very expensive phenomenon now-a-days. Investment has been directly proportional to income and then savings too out of necessary expenses. Where there is a large population which is not able to survive properly, needs to be ensured proper health services by state. India is among the many countries which despite its growing prosperity on economic and developmental fronts has the highest burden of malnutrition among its people in the world. Malnutrition adversely affects the health particularly among the children, right in the era of human rights movement. Malnutrition is the major factor which is responsible for about half of all the child deaths. Even the children who fortunately or unfortunately survive they suffer from serious physical and mental impairment. There are millions and millions of such children who fail to reach their youth. Their youth passes away in starving conditions. Continuously weak and weak due to unhealthy conditions they ultimately die. Nations are not in a position to utilize their potential for individual growth of such youth and for economic growth of the country itself.

For poor children the states have to strictly bring welfare policy basically in health care. To ensure adequate investment in healthcare it is not only the commitment on part of the national or state governments but this initiative should also be ignited from the side of the people as well. The children who are born in poor families they need support from the governments which are welfare states. Healthcare being provided by the private sectors may appear to be of a good level but it is not up to the reach of the poor people. The public sector healthcare services are not being rendered up to the mark for the reasons of bad governance. This is bitter truth and the governments must accept it as a challenge. Unless the governments handle them tough healthcare is not possible. Healthcare is most important dimension of human care. Let the governments do more for caring the human.

It is a big humanitarian issue and it must be of serious concern too, as to why our governments are so careless towards public health? Public health is a fundamental requirement. Do our governments need to make any separate planning for its protection? It is quite natural a thing that would there be human life if there is no health in it? If it is not healthy then how come such a society would survive? Did you ever examine the health policies of the states? You would get such societies on this earth whose childhood is hungry. Thus one could easily imagine as to how strong would be the youth of such society? Where some good health facilities would be available in either urban or metropolitan areas then only those would be benefitted who are economically capable and are in a position to bear the expenses relating to health. But such people are not much in numbers. Did you ever see the position of health facilities existing in our rural areas? Primary health centers in villages are in worst conditions and they almost remain closed. Medicines are not available. Essential infrastructures for treatment are not there. Doctors are seen appointed on papers only and never feel bothered to visit the centre regularly. They are absolutely fearless since administrative control is completely lacking. Such a kind of fearlessness is possible only due to mutual nexus with higher administrative officials. By remaining in the city of their choice they are busy in the profession of private medical practice. Once in a while when they feel like they would make a round of the primary health centre in the village where are posted. Rest of the healthcare is left on mercy of the God. This is not the way of human care. Forget about infrastructural medical facilities. When people would fall sick no treatment would be available. If they would think for better treatment then they would have no money. A society where people do struggle day and night to earn for their bread, if they are not out to work for the day then their family members would not have the bread to eat that night. They have no money in the form of any bank balance. In case fallen sick they would not be able to go out for work even. The children in the family would start starving. They go out to work in full sickness, if they do not earn where is the money for treatment of the sick? They have to look for the bread and not the butter, of the kids too. The sole bread earners of the family would go weak and weak under the circumstances. One fine morning they would be dead due to sickness and struggling for the bread. Kids would now be left behind only to starve and starve.

If we talk about human resource then poverty or prosperity could not be its parameters. Those who are prosperous definitely they would be able to worry for themselves and take extra care. Health related problems of people would adversely affect their physical and intellectual capacity to work. We would need to see the working capacity of our human resource linked with economic strength of our nation. Majority of human resource of our country is economically weak. Why we are not able to watch this bitter truth? It would be a matter of serious concern. If we are able to watch then definitely we are so carelessly in the habit of ignoring it. Then our intentions appear to be quite deliberate. This cannot be in any manner said to be a fair thing for betterment of our national healthcare system. Now we are seven decades old an independent nation. Seventy years time is not any short period that still we are not able to make available fundamental infrastructural health facilities to our citizen in remote urban, semi-urban and rural areas. This has gone to be a big mistake. Do we call it a blunder? It should be taken as a kind of warning to the caretakers of the nation that the majority human resource which keeps fighting with health related problems is victim of malnutrition. Such country could never be a strong nation since thinking about an overall development of the nation under prevailing circumstances would prove to be a myth.

Human health and human care could be two sides of the same coin. In its root human development would be significant. Prosperous countries of the world have given special priority to human care since they better understand that only the intellectual capacity of their citizen would help in making them a prosperous and strong nation. We need not to search for the reasons elsewhere if such nations are the leaders in the areas of science and research. Their achievements are the result of sustainable investment done by them in human care and health. India would also be making policies relating to human health and care which remain subject to effective enforcement at grass root levels. Need not to say policy enforcement rate in India in its true letters and spirit is very poor. This is good when reference of National Rural Health Mission (NRHM) comes. Completing formalities by merely making policies on paper would not serve the purpose. In India the face of corruption and scams is very fearful. Why a person should not doubt the intentions of the governments in the face of such corruptions? The governments fail to deal with such corruptions due to high profile levels of criminal nexus. Ministers in the governments also form part such nexus. After making health welfare policies on papers the funds are given at the disposal of those who bungle out the funds in the name of health policy investment. Do the governments are not aware of it? The governments are very much aware about it since the representatives of the government also do have their hands in glove with. This way the healthcare mission goes to shatters by compromising the most delicate part of human strength and their survival. We forget at the same time that we have compromised the strength of our nation too. It is very difficult and painful to understand but it happens. If the governments are not honest in strictly enforcing their own policies in the interest of human resource then it would prove to be a permanent loss to the nation. It is seen that either at investigation levels or going through technical complexities of the court proceedings the matters relating to policy investment scams by government officials in league with private contractors often collapses. Human resource is destroyed due to malnutrition. Who cares? Nation goes weak.

While I am expressing my concern for human healthcare the world is fighting its battle with Covid-19 all across the globe. Even the countries with much advanced infrastructural facilities like China, Italy, Spain and United States etc. are facing a big challenge from the novel corona virus. It would be a trying times to us the Indians for an honest introspection to enhance our healthcare capacities keeping this very fact in mind that according to government records around 30% of Indian population lives below the poverty line. Official data would reveal that such population are most sensitive and are worst sufferers of pandemic situations. Let us make our nation strong by increasing its immunity strength.

"Healthcare and human care are two sides of the same coin. In its root human development would be significant. Prosperous countries of the world have given special priority to human care

since they better understand that only the intellectual capacity of their citizen would help in making them a prosperous and strong nation. Their achievements are the result of sustainable investment done by them in human care and health."

26

HEALING FORCE OF MIND

We are the creatures of the universe. Our mind is the unique gift attributed to us by the universe. We need to understand our mind. Let us not ignore this fact that our mind has the strength and the capacity to create its own universe and start searching about the realities and the perpetual truth about the universe-the creator. Yes…!!! Universe of the mind unfolds the secrets of the universe by means of evolving its own evolutionary path. The mind participates while we search and research. It is for the reasons of this feature of mind that our scientists and researchers come out with conclusions in the form discoveries and inventions. Have you ever experienced the magical potency of mind? Potency in the sense that it mends itself even under acute adverse circumstances provided it has been nurtured with right kind of positive inputs.

Healing is a vital process of certain injury whether sustained physically or in any psychological form. Healing is an essential part under medical sciences for the purposes of proper mental and physical soundness. A healthy and strong mind controls and regulates a healthy human body. Therefore, there is a need to ensure with determination about the qualities of inputs or the virtues being supplied to the mind from the outer world. You are the master of your own virtues and finally to decide whether what nature of quality inputs need be allowed to enter your mind? While the rest worthless to be strictly filtered out so as to prevent your mind in getting polluted from the worldly dirt. Once pollution creeps in your mind for a permanency then make it a point that healing capacity of mind is going to be diminished and you will definitely lead towards mental sickness.

It is my observation that our mind is always positive to support us in our day to day mental processes unless we give it certain negative inputs. Supportive feature of mind was well understood by our all time great thinkers of the world so they could come out with abundant knowledge in welfare of the mankind on this earth. They could do what they were up to and they wanted to do. We need to understand the central role of mind in healing process. It is central to everything, every process and phenomenon. It is now up to us to supply the mind with quality fertile material continuously to get the expected results. The mind participates actively to start with healing process subject to the condition in a manner we respond to it. Spiritual condition is a stage of concentration of mind which takes us close to the nature and acts as a catalyst to the healing of self and the nature. Concentration of mind is possible when you are full with positive thoughts in your mind. You are thus able to create your own universe in due participation of mind towards ultimate happiness and fullness of life.

Healing force of a human mind has direct bearing with the spiritual power of a man. You would yourselves observe that when you are mentally disturbed you feel a kind of weakness from within. It appears as if your body has gone less with strength. Your strength has been reduced. If it happens that you feel lost by your mind then make it a point that as if you have lost the life too. Where your mind is strong, you have not lost your mind then you would be the sure winner. You could very easily notice that if a person is around with a depressed mind then it becomes very difficult for him to get himself out of it. The psychopath would no doubt provide him the treatment but he well understands that unless the man himself comes out with his supportive mind with positive thoughts it would be very difficult for the man to come out of rigorous stage of depression. The doctor would always keep advising the man that he should make his mind strong by thinking positive and reading healthy and creative literature. He should not allow negative thoughts to enter his mind. He also mentions that the medicines would only be effective when he is alert about positivity of his mind. The medicines would only support but ultimately the positive mind only would help the man to come out of depressed state. Otherwise the treatment would go on and the medicines simply would be of no use.

Healing power of the mind is very comprehensive. Healing requirements means when for any reason you are feeling physically and mentally weak for the reasons from within you. Healing power of the mind starts by processing of secretion of certain chemicals within your body. These chemicals would work like medicines to heal out your sickness. You need to understand the mechanism of bio-chemistry of your mind. Your physical weakness or any other such problem is due to defective bio-chemistry of your body. The resistance capacity of your body and mind is nothing but it is your bio-chemical balancing within your body system. The moment you allow negative thoughts in your mind this bio-chemical balancing in your body is disturbed. You start feeling not good. You should not look for the reasons of your defective bio-chemistry elsewhere. The reasons you would get around you only. How is your thinking? Did you ever examine that? Did you allow others to transfer their negativity to your mind? How did you feel looking to the success of others? You did not feel good. Or else, you felt good. If you felt good then he must be somebody close to you. If you were not happy by others success then you would have become jealous about him.

Happiness would make you cheerful, jealousy would make you dull. You would irritate like following dullness. You would have definitely experienced such moments in your life on one point of time or the other. Whenever you feel happy then on directions of your mind the body system starts secretion of beneficial chemicals within you which made you cheerful and full with joy. Obviously, you will continue to be cheerful and happy till your mind keeps supplying such beneficial chemical to your body. After all, who does not want to be happy in his life? The life objective of human has been to keep happy and peace of mind. Why does the jealousy make you sadistic because you were not able to be happy by the success of others? For not being happy your mind stopped secreting the chemicals which make you happy. It is an auto-regulated physical and chemical process which remains subject to the person keeping happy. Your jealous thinking started inducing your mind to secret harmful chemicals so under the influence of it you are not able to keep yourself happy. You feel sad and worried about. Further as it commonly happens when effect of harmful chemicals continues long then you come under depression. Acute depression would be the condition indicating large quantity of harmful chemicals collected in your body. It would not be a good thing for you. If it prolongs further then it may turn to be dangerous even. Your supportive mind would heal entire depressive conditions provided you supplied it with positive thoughts so that mind signals for secretion of beneficial chemicals within your body to counter with harmful chemicals already in your body. You start feeling good and happy because continuous supply of beneficial chemicals due to positive thoughts has generated tuning of bio-chemical balancing in your body. Your mind supported you the maximum in this healing process of your depression.

You will have to be happy otherwise you are going to spoil your life. Now your problem is as to how to get rid of the effect of harmful jealously induced chemicals? It would not be possible all of a sudden by any medicine or medical treatment unless the healing force of your mind helps you out. It would be possible when the beneficial chemicals being secreted in the state of happiness and good thoughts are able to outdo and destroy the effect of jealously induced harmful chemicals inside your body. Your mind would participate by means of destroying the bad effect of harmful chemicals. With the help of its healing force it would increase quantities of beneficial chemicals. But it would only be possible when under the directions of your mind the quantity of beneficial chemicals becomes on higher side as compared to the quantity of jealously induced chemicals. But this is not going to happen overnight. The longer duration your mind remained under depression it would take at least that much or a bigger duration to get rid you off it. Secretions of beneficial chemicals would depend upon the length of duration you remain happy with positive thoughts. Your longer happy state of mind only would make you cheerful again and again. Medicinal chemicals are already present in your body positive as well as negative. Recognize the healing force of your mind. It is for this reason that the mind which remained subject to positivity it remained healthy. You may happen to receive some physical wounds or cuts in your body. You find that you are able to cure such wounds without recourse to medical treatment. The bio-chemistry of your body system possesses internal mechanism to fight with external germs in curing the wounds or cuts. As soon your any body part is wounded your mind receives pain signals first. We always call for better immunity within our body. The immunity system of our body is controlled by our mind. You might have read the real stories of fights back where person found suffering from painful ailments and doctors struggling day and night to provide the best medical treatment to them. The doctors getting disappointed as they do not find themselves to cure the ailment subject to medical sciences prescriptions. The team of doctors communicates the patient about their helplessness with a very heavy heart. The healing power of the mind strikes with unparallel exhibition of mind will power. The patient in few days comes out with recovery signs to the utmost surprise of doctors. The person ultimately cures himself fit by healing touch of the mind and by its will power. Healthy body and minds live great and do great.

"You could very easily notice that if a person is around with a depressed mind then it becomes very difficult for him to get himself out of it. The psychopath would no doubt provide him the treatment but he well understands that unless the man himself comes out with his supportive mind with positive thoughts it would be very difficult for the man to come out of rigorous stage of depression. The doctor would always keep advising him to think positive, read positive and avoid negative thoughts."

27

YOUR SPIRITUAL STRENGTH

You are honest, feeling to be accountable and kind enough to the people around you. Off course, by means of these virtues you will attain inner strength. But do you ever feel that once you have acquired these virtues then you forget about the existence of the Almighty in the universe and start considering yourself to be all powerful. Keep remembering Godly existence of the Almighty is quite an essential component to enhance your spiritual strength within. If you do not care to include spiritual realities in your life only for the reasons that you are honest, truthful, accountable and kind then make it a point that you are not going to be a 'spiritual man'. You will lose all the strength you acquired by practicing those virtues. You are incomplete in the sense that you are spiritually a weak person.

Wellness of your physical body has nothing to do with your spiritual strength. Beyond a certain point your physical wellness fails you unless you possess the spiritual strength. That is the universal truth that every action in this nature has an equal and opposite reaction. Every loss has to be balanced by a gain. Life always experiences fluctuations from one extreme to the other. A stage comes in life that things do not materialize in right manner the way people wanted to be. Life is not always an upwards movement it has it's downwards movement too. Problems arise to handle such situations unless we have learnt to live with calm and peace. Such calmness at the centre of our body is not possible without the spiritual strength.

Spiritual strength is generated in unison with yourself and the Almighty in meditation. I believe in existence of an invisible force which controls and regulates the nature and the environment we all live in. You have the ego of being honest and being kind. Your this ego are the obstacles which you need to give up in order being in unison with the Almighty. Let your body and your life belong to the Almighty. Let the Almighty transform you into him. It is impossible unless you allow him so to do for you. You want nothing for yourself but the Almighty. Being in unison with the Almighty is nothing but an extreme state of calm and peaceful mind. Spiritual strength causes wonders in you in the form of self-giving and the resultant calmness which follows. Attainment through meditation is not an overnight phenomenon. It is your inward giving up though a continuous process of devotion and meditation which ultimately will make one feel an attainment of spiritual strength with an outward reflection on your face, your body and day to day movement.

Tragedies, sufferings are to follow in human life. But these make no difference to the people who have attained spiritual attunement through perpetual unison with the Almighty. That is the real spiritual strength. Do you ever feel this thing when you appear to be weak by your spiritual power? You can think this even that it would not be that easy to get oneself liberated from day to day worldly life. Can we be a spiritual strength by continuing to be into worldly life? Or if the spiritual strength is to be achieved then one need to leave worldly life. Further questions would arise out of such questions. Whether to be worldly or renounce this world? Keeping honest and then not feeling proud to be honest. Keeping healthy means to keep stay within one self. Spiritual philosophy never preconditions to renounce this world. In a society with full of dishonest characters if an honest person becomes self-pride then what is wrong in it. Why his self feel of proud appears to be objectionable to others? Or else such feel of pride goes to create hurdles in his spiritualistic achievements? Why do we tend to forget that spiritual strength exists within the human being itself? Self pride of a man is subject only to the control of his inner strength. Probably the kind of self pride would have appeared appropriate to the spiritual power under the circumstances. Person's integrity also confers him with internal strength. In present manipulative kind of socio-economic perspectives maintaining integrity is becoming quite challenging for a person. Majority of people with dishonest characters consider the person with integrity to be an obstacle and a man full with fear. People start telling him since he cannot be dishonest is a weak hearted person. He is having no courage to be dishonest that is why he plays to be honest and shows integrity. Such kind of talks among people would definitely discourage him because in such a corrupt system he would be thrown alone. But the person should never think like that. He should never forget that the kind of spiritual strength he has conserved due to his integrity, it would not be possible for the dishonest people in majority to destroy that strength. Need not to repeat that honesty is the best policy indeed.

World history has been witness to this fact that the conspiracies to hang and put to death honest and truth tellers had been designed none else but by majority of dishonest bad characters only. But the bad characters could not deter spirituality of such great men even for a bit and could not finish out their existence on this earth. In almost all periods honest persons with full integrity are put to rigorous tests by the people with bad and dishonest characters. It sounds strange but a bitter truth. When hundreds of dishonest characters are seen compelled to collect together to finish the existence of an honest one then it could be easily understood and imagined the spiritual power of such a person. But the very painful question comes out of it whether in all periods the honest ones are only to be hanged? Whether the dishonest characters that happen to be larger in number would succeed in keep making their vicious designs to finish men with honesty and values? Whether the honesty only in all ages would be put to rigorous trials by the majority with dishonesty? Who would give reply to these questions after all? Reply to these questions is not going to be that easy. But their spiritual strength would be testimony to this fact that such great men survived on this earth through ages despite they were put to death by dishonest bad characters. If these few honest characters were not on this earth with full strength of their spirituality then the humanity on this earth would have been destroyed since long. This world in fact is balancing on the strength of these few honest characters only if you so wish you can see around.

In what way you connect the power of Almighty and spirituality? Almighty power must be seen as a power in comprehensive balancing of the nature. We feel that unlimited power which regulates this nature. The sun, sky, earth, seas, rivers, mountains, vegetations, flora-fauna, wind, storm hurricanes, cooling, rains, climate, atmosphere, environment and within all that our human existence and our spirituality. Our nearer one, strangers, getting something, loosing something, happiness, pleasure, sorrow, worry, jealousy, sadistic pleasure, anger benevolence, positive, negative, ego, violence, greed, dishonesty, honesty, truth, lie, pain, joy and lot many mutually contradictory human perceptions. Has there been any occasion in your life when nature would have automatically made you realize about Godly presence? Natural Godly power would have been straightway visible before you. When hurricanes are to come the inventions of science cannot stop them. Hurricanes would move with its devastations then science would rescue whatever has been left behind. The Covid-19 has been multiplying its toll through its various stages all across the world while medical sciences have completely surrendered before the novel virus. Science has its own limits, the nature has much more. Would you ever see the shape of God? Some image which you could fix on your mind screen? Accept this you would have heard people telling that some invisible force is there which runs this nature. How wonderful, how powerful and how spiritualistic? Almighty…!!! You would only feel with the depth of your mind. This Godly power is going to stay within your mind. You cannot spare yourself. Your physical existence is also made up by these components of nature only and one day you would be vanished within this nature. Could you see how closely you are connected with the Godly power of your nature? For these reasons only you endowed with spiritualistic characters in yourself. Whether by living in worldly life or by going out of it, nobody can separate your spirituality from the Almighty. You have become absolutely complete you would feel about.

"Life always experiences fluctuations from one extreme to the other. A stage comes in life that things do not materialize in right manner the way people wanted to be. Life is not always an upwards movement it has it's downwards movement too. Problems arise to handle such situations unless we have learnt to live with calm and peace. Such calmness at the center of our body is not possible without the spiritual strength."

28

YOU - THE WINNER

Every person has a deep instinct within to be a winner. Winners also are just like ordinary persons on this earth. Winners are not born but they are made by subjecting themselves through rigorous process of psychological and physical training and practice. One should never think about that the winners are gifted with something extra-ordinary. But they make themselves extra-ordinary by sincerely and continuously putting some extra efforts than ordinary. Almighty has gifted every individual equally. The winners are different in the sense that they practice their gift to the maximum with a deep urge to become successful. And they succeed ultimately. Have you watched practicing those athletes who are Olympic winners? Have you seen deep through their eyes? Their body language is talking tough full with self confidence. This did not happen overnight you understand. Looking to their achievement across the world we think that they were born with some special gift. We watch world class artists working upon their masterpieces. We think of their talents as if they are born artists. We see billionaires of the world who remain on top of the rich list. Why do we wonder? Do they become rich par chance? Let us not talk about corrupt politicians, businessmen, government officials getting billionaires overnight. This tendency of corruption has ruined the moral fabric of society and has completely damaged the bonds of human relationships on the earth. Learning negative tendencies among human being is very fast. It is very rare that people desire to pass through a rigorous hard process to achieve success particularly when there are examples available around them people becoming billionaires overnight by resorting to corrupt dishonest means. The tragedy above all is that the existing criminal justice system completely fails in preventing such corrupt practices and the culprits move on without any trace of fear on their faces. Their closeness with law enforcement they feel cannot punish them. This trend encourages the new learners of such dishonest tendencies in the society. This proves to be a bad signal for winners who ultimately feel discouraged about their sincere efforts in an environment of corrupts and dishonesty.

The winners should not be discouraged and lose their heart. It is only camping on the moral strength of the winners that this earth survives despite all odds and becomes a place worth to live in. You make out some time to minutely examine the attitude of winners. You will find them honest by heart. They cannot be corrupt and dishonest at any cost come what may. Their attitude makes them determine that the moment they cease to be honest they cease to be winners. They are made of such a metal only that they are not deterred by corrupt and dishonest tendencies prevalent in any society in any period of time. How to be a winner? It should not be difficult question. Winners are also just like any other ordinary person. But they are mentally tough. Their mental strength is the result of a continuous practice through perseverance. They refuse to be ordinary. Winners refuse to do anything which is ordinary. This attitude only makes them extra-ordinary. You too will be the winner provided that you put yourself to the tough practice to reach to the same mental level and to be the same metal the winners are made of. What makes a winner's attitude? People who have attained success in life and have put in a long journey full with obstacles make the attitude of a winner. They are not known to be losers and even in their failures they emerge to be winners. It was not an easy track for them to move on. They put in tremendous amount of efforts to reach to the point of height where they are today.

Winners are not born success but they are born only to succeed. They never give up in their effort making that is the secret they succeed on. Success is not a kind of gift for an individual but it is made through and earned tough. The champions winning tournaments in world class athletics, Olympics etc. have to perform within fraction of seconds only to win the gold medal along with other world class competitors. To perform within fraction of seconds during tournaments the winners have to keep on rigorous practice for years and years altogether nonstop. It is not that all of sudden they emerge to be the champions of the game. Winners are made. Their determination makes them winners. Their mental attitude and will power makes them winners. You would be seeing a person who is a billionaire today. But you may never see and came to know about his many failures and business losses for years while he was struggling through. He passed through tedious painful process of becoming a billionaire today. Experience his state of mind then he suffered a series of losses in business before he became rich. He could have gone insane and mentally unsound. How could have he maintained his mental balance? He would have been disappointed absolutely due to his successive failures. He would have thought of to give up in between but he never gave up despite losses and failures. He controlled himself and became mentally strong to cope up with adversities. Yes…!!! Today he is a billionaire. One should not feel envious about him instead of get inspired. You can also be the winner by constantly developing the winner's attitude and keep performing with full of your efforts and capacity.

Material attainment is completely different from spiritual attainment. To be a winner in material life does not mean to be a winner spiritually as well. You need to be a winner in spiritual sense too. What do you feel to be the ultimate goal for yourself in your human life? In last phases of their life despite all material successes people desire to be champions in strict spiritual sense so that they are able to win their own self. Can you win yourself? Did you not see people who are materially sound but still they do not feel to be happy in their life? They clamor for calm and peace. They understand that no kind of money is going to buy peace of mind for them. They keep on visiting from one religious place to the other in search of peace of mind. But of no avail. Spiritual winning situation is very close to us. We are not able to achieve this because we do not have a still mind. We have a mind which keeps roaming around for material gains instead. What we need is that not only to still our mind but make it to stay focused within its own self. Our outer world is big enough to distract our mind and thoughts from our inner world. Why do we talk about a focused mind? This question arises when you are materially sound but still you do not feel yourself to be the winner. You understand that your money would not be able to buy the peace of mind for you. When money is not able to help you out then you feel yourself to be the looser. Now your money appears to be of no use for you. You do not want to be the looser at any cost since you have a winner's attitude. Now you are ready to leave your all money for the sake of peace of mind and the spiritual pleasure. Here comes the real winner from within. You will be the winner of your life while leaving behind your hard earned money for the sake of the mankind.

Look here. Material success is not bad by any standard provided that the material has been earned by putting in hard work and honestly. You want to be a rich man by earning money. You desire to be a rich man by earning knowledge. Both are two different things. Earning money by dishonest means would put you in trouble one day. May be you are able to escape punishment and managed to run away from the clutches of laws of the land but never forget that your children are going to spoil their life by the money you earned badly and by unlawful means. This would be the biggest punishment for you in your life. Where goes the winner? You have reached to a point of no return. You would not be left even worth repenting. You have lost the game of your life. The money you earned honestly and by lawful means would give you the needed strength to live a winner. You would be able to win for your family a life full with values and virtues. It would give you a miraculous strength when you would come forward to help out the needy from the money you earned by putting in hard work. Now even hundreds of distractions that keep pulling your attention would not be able to disturb you in any manner. Experience the inner peace and bliss. Yes…!!! Winners are not born they are made through patience and perseverance with a never give up attitude. It would not be a tough task for you to make your attitude with the needed mindset that you are born to win.

"Winners are also just like any other ordinary person. But they are mentally tough. Their mental strength is the result of a continuous practice through perseverance. They refuse to be ordinary. Winners refuse to do anything which is ordinary. This attitude only makes them extra-ordinary. You too will be the winner provided that you put yourself to the tough practice to reach to the same mental level and to be the metal winners are made from."

29

YOU THINK YOU OWN

The concept of ownership is particularly good in property related matters. The person who is the owner of a thing it is not necessary that he is in possession of that thing also. The big question may arise when a person does not even possess a thing can he own it? The concept may hold good for purposes of jurisprudential studies but when it comes to possession of certain ideas or feelings its application is going to be quite different under changing situations.

Possession of a thing is a feeling. That is animus possession. If you possess a thought you own a thought. You may feel that you are the owner of your intellectual property. You are the owner of your wife and the children. Have you ever felt that whether you possess them? Do you ever feel that the feeling of possessiveness within you creates a kind of compulsive impulse on the things you own or the thoughts you generate? Can you compel any person that he should succumb to your compulsive impulse and be in your possession? Are you able to possess your own self honestly? If not, then how would you be able to possess others, who are not within your control? Let them be your wife your children or other people related to you.

Meaning thereby, whether what you think you own or not is completely dependent upon perception of other people. You would be said to own your ideas and thoughts, if you are able to exactly pronounce them or practice them in their true letters and spirit. If you are not able to translate your ideas and thoughts into your life style in practice and in your behavior then you are not the owner of your thoughts. Ownership and possession are mutually related concepts. You first are the owner of your thoughts and ideas then think of possessing them in perpetuity. If the things or the people we feel to possess leave us away then our perception of ownership is gone.

Feeling of possessiveness is painful for the human beings because it is completely banking upon outwardly things. The real owner is the person who thinks and assimilates in his life style without bothering for physical possession of the things. Make sure that you will be truly possessive when the possession of things is not dependent upon others things. You will be truly happy and peaceful in your mind. Ownership is not bad nor did the possession provided you are able to possess yourself, own yourself. This is in true sense called as the concept of non-possessiveness. This does not mean to give up the things but to attain them with inner completeness. Realization of your own self is the complete possession and you start feeling them practicing in your life style that what you think you own.

This thought must be coming to your mind that why the feeling of rights comes within you? Who has the right to possess certain thoughts or having the right to ownership over such thoughts? How could this be possible if one is the owner of what he was thinking? Yet another thought could be that whether the person could actually own of what he thinks whether he is in possession of it or not? To look for answers to these thoughts would prove to be quite analytical. When thoughts are made subject to research we find there are many relevant modifications and improvement suggested by the researchers. One idea could be relevant in a particular time space then the author may well own such ideas in that space only. Not only time space but it may vary from one region to the other in the same time space. Later on it is noticed that old ideas are found to have lost its utility with changing generations. Suppose we have ideas about human relation thoughts on human liberties. With changing civilizations the perspectives of concept of liberties keep changing. The champions of liberties at one point of time become obsolete at another point of time. Do we become owner of human liberties merely by such thoughts? We may own and possess but we should keep ready to relinquish such possessions when they are found to be out of practice under prevalent situations. It is nature born desire of a person that what he owns looks for its possession as well. People must understand that their life span is limited. They think they can own during their life time only provided they kept putting it into practice. It depends upon cementing force of your thoughts that later generations find it relevant to be carried into practice even after your life time. Let the generations be the owners of your ideas and introduce modifications in them depending upon their future needs. Subject to their necessities the future generations would be in position to modify such ideas only when they own it. They possessed the ideas but when they put those ideas into their day to day behavior they are now able to own those ideas. Thus they become able to modify such ideas, by virtue of the fact that they own, subject to future changing needs. One cannot wish to compel people so that they keep making one feel to be the owner. Your compulsive impulse of ownership should have been that it suggests initiatives to get rid of the people from their countless problems being hunger and poverty at the top. Yes…!!! They too would have to make efforts for their pathetic conditions. They are able to make efforts and are getting proper remedy of it. A kind of such environment needs to be created based upon socialistic pattern of governance. Those who are in power must come forward with thoughts to help all equally without discrimination as what they mean they own it.

There is a thought of equality of opportunity. This thought has been enshrined in law books of nations as well. It is to be owned not on individual basis but is supposed to be carried forward under state ownership. What a constitutional government thinks it must own it. People with hunger know that if they would not work hard then they would die. There are researches which reveal that governments have badly failed in conferring equality of opportunity to its people. The thought may appear to be good and sound on papers but when seen down to earth it lacks its force. So the governments possess the thoughts but they do not own it. Once the governments what think they own too the governance goes on its top level. You can then feel the prosperity, economic and psychological strength of any nation. Had there been the equality of opportunity then there would have been clear prosperity in the society? Why do not we all become the owners of similar thoughts? Everybody would like a prosperous society. But thoughts merely would not do. We need to be their owners as well. Meaning thereby when thoughts come down to the level of ground realities then only could be seen the strength of compulsory impulses of your ownership.

What you think you own that is good. But how could your good thought be limited to you only? It should not be. Our present society is passing through an acute moral crisis. The social character and political behavior has also been downgraded. Your good thoughts would make place in minds of the people. They would feel that their life has become enlightened. The inspiration of your ideas would make them to do all that which you aspire to be done for the benefit of the society. They would feel pleasure with themselves. The social happiness vests in their happiness. Not only all the people would possess your ideas in the society but they would become the owners of your ideas too since they have your ideas into their habits. They would also start putting in their efforts by converting your ideas into reality so as to make this society prosperous and happy. It would only be possible when every person in the society comes forward with a determination that he would become the owner of good ideas and healthy thoughts. You can experience your strong will power, life full with meaning and your happiness levels unlimited. You feel that you have achieved the purpose for you were born on this earth. There was no more enmity with anyone. You were the reason for it. Then all those who were inspired by your ideas became owners of your thoughts. Possibly it would only be the extremity of your pleasure and social happiness. The perspective of the global happiness would also be like it only. It could happen because what people came out to think they could own and they could transfer ownership of thoughts from one generation to the other and even could improve upon them in the larger good of mankind.

"It depends upon cementing force of your thoughts that future generations find it relevant to be carried into practice even after your life time. Let the generations be the owners of your ideas and introduce modifications in them depending upon their future needs. Subject to their necessities the future generations would be in a position to modify such ideas only when they own it. They possessed the ideas but when they put those ideas into their day to day behavior now they are able to own those ideas."

30

FEAR MOTIVATES YOU

Fear factor is very significant in personality of any individual. We have the feeling of fear consciousness in our day to day behavior. We are afraid as to what we should do and what we should not? We also have the fear whether we should go to a particular place or we should not? We regularly have an impact of fear in our mind of some kind or the other. We do not start with our lot many activities for fear of getting failure. We have the fear of rejection that is why we fail to speak well before the interview board. Fear consciousness deprives us from lot many achievements. We perceive that had the fear not been there, it would have been easy for us to achieve things the way we wanted them to be.

Fearfulness is a common psychological state of mind in every person. It moves forward by a thought process for balancing mechanism of the human body against warranted or unwarranted human emotions. It is so natural within survival process of our body system that we just cannot avoid it. The only way out to handle it is to keep ready to face the fear. Catch the fear and throw it away. We need to develop a kind of mechanism in biological system of our body so that we overcome the fear and learn to live with it. Once we are able to attain mastery over fear the magnitude of our success will be much higher. Our expert psychologists are very clear about the concept of fear. Fear possesses a great driving force and at the same time if we are able to honestly perceive the fear it proves to be a great motivator to us. The fear in true sense musters extra potential from within the human body to face adversities of the life. Now it is for us to develop mental preparedness to utilize our internal fear potential to meet out our day to day fear challenges.

Allowing fear to continuously remain in subconscious mind is very dangerous. It badly affects the body and the mind. It is not only a great motivator at times but at the same time it causes stress also even to the extent of damaging your nervous system. We should never forget that source of fear is always within us only and for this we are only to be blamed. Any external stimulus is merely a causative factor for inducing fear in our mind. Now it is up to our mental strength if we allow such external stimulus to engulf our mind with fear. Instead fear overpowers us, we need to face the fear and overcome it. Yes...!!! We should remember that death is a certain fear but still we make ourselves mentally prepared to face it with courage. We need to develop motivation from certain fear of death. One of the most potent ways to tackle with perception of fear is that law of action. You can experience that till you are lying idle with inaction the fear catches your mind like anything and pulls you down. Once you start with to act upon, fear automatically diminishes. Always make up your mind that there is nothing to fear. This should be your mindset. To repeat fear is again a state of mind. Once you are able to set this state of mind in a right manner fear disappears and you will march towards your goal fearlessly.

Why to be worried about from fear at all? We know it fully well that fear psychology makes people weak not only mentally but physically as well. Who are the people, who are not affected by fear psychosis at all? Understand that they are not any kind of super human beings. They are also ordinary people just like us only. They did not become fearless overnight. It is their logical observation of happening of chain of events around them that they are able to make a mindset to encounter with the fear head on. You will not be able to free yourself from the fear psychosis unless you examine the chain of events in your life with a logical mind. Logic has been based upon scientific analysis of existing facts relating to any happening in your life like failure. People believe in superstitious practices without scaling them on the parameters of logic or reasoning. Do religious beliefs enhance superstitious tendencies lacking no logic or reason? They are based upon imaginary thoughts of a particular religious community. It is often heard people saying that religions make human beings fearful. We should remember that religions teach us to be a better human being, respect emotions of fellow human beings, practice brotherhood as a human being. Then who stops you from practice all this? Where is lack of logic or reason? Be a better human being. No religion permits the kind of superstitious practices we come across in our society. Treat your fellow human being as your brother. What is there to fear about all that? But still we remain scared about. Why...??? No religion existing on this earth teaches you to hate your fellow human beings. Why we fear since we hate? All is not well in and around your society. People are looked down upon and even killed in the name of religion. You fear because your intentions are not good and are absolutely full with guilty consciousness. Try to look into yourself thorough deep.

You cannot ignore this very fact that the traces of fear consciousness lie within you only. There are people who are able to exploit your mind make you full with fear. Because they know that you are sensitive and have a fear tendency. A person would always have a kind of fear who possesses dishonest intention. May be he is able to suppress the signs of fear for certain moment but a stage comes when he is not able to control himself and his fear outbursts. His capacity to suppress his fear crosses the limit. He is scared when he intends to cause certain injury to somebody. He knows that his conduct is wrongful. You might have witnessed hardened criminals out there seeking mercy and begging for their life is spared. It is seen that the so-called caretakers of religion exploit innocent emotions of religious minded people. Considering religion to be supreme codes of conduct persons of such religious community look determined to follow them strictly. They fear of the idea that by no means they should violate that. Being innocently they commit mistakes. The caretakers put a kind of fear in the mind of people that if they are not performing such and such practice then they will suffer harm physical or moneywise. Some near and dear in the family would meet with an accident. Any beloved person may die also. This is the kind of fear people are encountering in the name of religious beliefs. The caretakers would frighten them and exploit them. This is criminal. But the social weakness is that people themselves are subjecting them to such criminal acts of the caretakers of such religions. They are not able to oppose them. Keep ready to face the fear. Fear is nothing but a creation of your mind generated from your weak ideas and the scared mindset. Your religion should not make you weak but it must make you strong. Always believe in yourself and move forward with a determined steps. Take help of the religion you believe in. It will show you the path you should move under given circumstances. You will find no trace of fear in your life. Natural happenings in your life are just challenges for you. This so happens in everybody's life. Never forget that every problem has its own solutions. You will not be able to get up to the solutions unless you act upon your problems firmly. You need to face them and handle them head on without fear. You cannot afford to sit with your fingers crossed doing nothing and expecting desired results for. Fear is a natural psychological and bio-chemical process in every living organism. It is quite natural then to understand that for countering this process you would need to develop your internal bio-chemical mechanism too in equal proportions to neutralize the fear psychology. Fear thus motivates you in the sense that it offers a challenge before you to either fight it out or surrender before it. Your mind accepted the challenge and started readiness with internal bio-chemical mechanism to attack the fear chemicals. Make sure that you are going to have a certain win against the fear since you decided not to surrender before it. You are motivated to fight it again on the strength of the immunity you have developed against fear. Those who could not muster the courage to fight the fear and instead they surrendered are certain to lose the battle of life. When you face the fear it makes you strong from within. So whenever there is fear situations in your life accept them as opportunities to strengthen yourself. A stage will finally come in your life that you find yourself so equipped and fear proof that you are no more scared of fears. Keep motivating yourself from fear it works.

"Our expert psychologists are very clear about the concept of fear. Fear possesses a great driving force and at the same time if we are able to honestly perceive the fear it proves to be a great motivator to us. The fear in true sense musters extra potential from within the human body to face adversities of the life. Now it is for us to develop mental preparedness to utilize our internal fear potential to meet our day to day fear challenges."

31

LIFE GIVES OPTIONS TO CHOOSE

It is not always necessary that the life is full of options. But this is confirmed that life gives options to choose. If we are alert enough to avail our options at right point of time then we are benefitted otherwise we are bound to be losers due to lost opportunities. It depends upon person to person and also depending upon the efforts they are making honestly to grab those opportunities. Those who are looking for options without making sincere efforts they would be losers. No doubt despite making good efforts there are people who have fewer choices. While there are people who have in abundance do not need to make much efforts. It is a system fault which needs to be cured by political regimes. Among whatever options available under any existing circumstances one always has a freedom of choice to choose that option which he feels to be better one for his overall good.

Today in the materialistic world people create options for themselves on the strength of their money power. Those with less money power or no money power virtually have no options. This no doubt happens to be a bitter truth. They have to accept whatever comes to them or they have to satisfy with nothing. In the event of no option available there is no freedom of choice. You have to accept it as it is whether good or bad. Why not to think of creating more options so that you have a freedom of choice for the better one? You may argue that practically it is not possible to create options at one's own free will. Your argument is sustained but by making sincere efforts in right directions and at a right point of time options can open up better avenues. You are free to apply your mind to choose the better one. It is not always the money which opens better avenues but it is your untiring labor and intellect too which possesses the same potential as any money can have. All are not rich it does not mean that only the rich would have multiple options.

There are situations that more options create more confusion. The confusion is that which one to choose particularly when all options appear to be equally better from your point of view. Really now this is going to be a very typical situation for you with multiple options all better ones and the freedom of choice at the same time. Always remember that freedom infuses responsibility. Any of your choice going bad you have to accept your responsibility without blaming others. Choosing without confusion is directly dependent upon clarity of your mind. Mind acts as a balance to weigh the multiple options. Intelligent application of your mind will help you choose the best option and win over the confusion. We want choice without confusion. In fact confusion is in our mind because of lack of clarity. Make sure that you are not going to apply your freedom of choice arbitrarily. It is completely up to you. But once you make a choice its final till you have another better option. You have to accept the consequences.

There is a saying that the beggars are not choosers. They have no choices. That is alright. The beggars are those who do not like to work or make any efforts to create choices for them. How come then they would be choosers? Life also does not promote any such tendency to be any chooser without work done. So if majority of beggars are not choosers then they are to be blamed for that. But when you are able to make a situation for yourself by putting in work so that you have the freedom of choice intending that what you wish to get then definitely you will be the chooser. However, this situation is not that easy the way we understand. Freedom of choice is not demanded it is commanded by a rightful person. You need to pass through a rigorous process to earn this freedom. That is true that in the materialistic world of today money matters. But one should not forget at the same time that it is not the case that money only always matters. People may have earned money by wrongful means. No doubt, they would be able to buy opportunities and freedoms despite the fact knowing it fully well that they are not eligible to enjoy such freedoms. This clearly goes to prove that merit would be ignored and suppressed. Knowledge has power is a very famous proverb. A person who believes in merit he would concentrate for merit only. He earns knowledge so he earns merit. Earning knowledge is also a very rigorous process. People in this world are seen sacrificing their entire life in search of knowledge and merit. Earning knowledge is not always necessary to be directly proportional to become rich as well. You may come across such scholars whose economic condition is quite bad in modern materialistic world. Question arises then where is the freedom of choice for such scholars? The scholars would also like to be rich because money is essential to survive. Are they destined to be hand to mouth for the only reasons that they kept on earning knowledge and not the money? Their knowledge no doubt helps but not sufficient enough in this materialistic world. They lack the freedom to choose to be rich by virtue of their knowledge. Yes…!!! This happens to be very pathetic situation.

There are meritorious students in our society who are poor and belong to weaker sections. Their talent is not going to help them out in earning the needed knowledge to survive in this competitive world since their parents do not have much money to buy any such support so that they can prepare themselves to face the world and buy opportunities for themselves. Like good living, healthy life and better educational facilities. They show their merit under very adverse and exceptional circumstances proving the fact that money is not bar. But this happens in rarest of the rare cases because of extra ordinary merit the student possesses. Creating more options for you so that your choice becomes much easier is also dependent upon you. But this would again be possible where a person possesses sufficient resources to proceed with.

We find our young generations in large numbers possessing technical and professional degrees who are struggling for better job opportunities. Unemployment is on big scale. Jobs are much less in number whereas claimants are plenty. Looking to this tough competition ahead there is no meaning of freedom of choice. Suppose freedom has been given to all but choices are limited then only limited one are benefitted. A youth may be better qualified gets a job which is much below the level of his qualification. He is forced to accept and satisfy with the job what he gets. A prevalent condition of job scarcity makes all the difference. It hampers the very enthusiasm of our youth to work on in accordance with their merit. Their output goes dismal with the passage of time. Job scarcity diminishes the chances of freedom of choice to our youth which is akin to their qualification and future scope of their merit application. We face then brain drain when our youth moving across the globe in search of better job options. Yes...!!! They do since we fail to provide them the level and quality of resources and infrastructure they need to enhance their meritorious skills. Our nation is not benefitted by their merit. Why do not we see it as a glaring failure on our part? We fail to provide them the much needed freedom of choice within our nation itself up to the level of their technical knowledge. Resultantly we are not a rich nation. We need to make our youth feel that there would be enough freedom of choice to all variety of options open for them so that they can apply their freedom in its true sense. I would like to emphasize at this stage that despite job insufficiencies your knowledge which you possess is your real strength. Make it a point that your knowledge is never wasted over any point of time. Despite the fact that existing system fails in providing you sufficient and better opportunities the potential of your knowledge is going to earn for you the space where you in fact deserve to be. Keep performing according to your merit in proving your best capacity to work. Life is going to ensure that you have options open knocking right at doorsteps. Always be judicious in choosing them not only for yourself but for the strength of your society and nation too.

"You may argue that practically it is not possible to create options at one's own free will. Your argument is sustained but by making sincere efforts in right directions at right point of time options can open up better avenues. You are free to apply your mind

to choose the better one. It is not always the money which opens better avenues but it is your untiring labor and intellect too which possesses the same potential as any money can have. All are not rich it does not mean that only the rich would have multiple options."

32

YOU HAVE LIFE TO LIVE

Do you ever take time to see that how do you live your life? And that you live your life the way you like it be. Are you sure that your life is exactly up to your likings or disliking? Are you not? Then it would be very difficult for you to say that you are living your life the way you like it. We also feel that our children should live their life the way we like it. You have already lived your life now you want to live the life of your children as well. Now this is the real question. Do we have any right to live life of others? And if we try to do so then to what extent it is going to be against the nature? Whether it would have some adverse implications also? It has adverse implications then we need to properly address to them.

Undoubtedly, one may argue that well meaning parents do have all good intentions for the sake of their children just with a view to see that they are not off the right track. They are cautioned well in time so that they choose their right career they wish to be. It could be a debatable issue as to whether to a fullest extent they are satisfied with their future what they have? Or it could have still been a better future, had they been permitted to live their own life. Keeping in mind the concept of inalienable rights of individuals not only in a social system but in family system as well such natural rights should not be denied. Not that we are not aware of it but still we try to take away the life of individuals for well justifiable reasons. Undoubtedly, every child has been conferred with basic right to decide their way of life to live but it is suggested that elderly advice in their way of life would make them more confident and result oriented.

The chief objective of one's life should be to perform such actions which are in search of pleasure and peace and not such actions which lead to worries in human life. Moral philosopher Immanuel Kant had his well intentioned advocacy for morality and ethics leading towards absolute fulfillment of universal human rights initiatives in favor of betterment of mankind. While the individuals should not be denied from their right to live at the same time this should also be advisable that they should reasonably think over elderly suggestions which are based upon their life experiences and which could save youngsters from any possible harm. Yes...!!! This should be an admitted fact that children definitely lack in practical life experiences. Trial and error could best be opted but it could prove to be a time wasting device. Learning by doing flavored with elder's experiences is going to be the best option.

What could be the expectations of our young generations in existing situations? If their expectation is progressive then there must be no worry about it. Deciding the scale of their progressiveness would be a challenging issue. We need to essentially examine the level of education we are going to provide them as on today. Education of children starts right from their home. Moral education would be conferred to them by their parents themselves. For school and other education the children would have to go out of home. Lot many things other than proper education the children would learn from outside which may not be according to their family atmosphere. It would be a genuine worry of the parents that their children should keep away from bad habits when they are away from home. Definitely it is going to be a big challenge. The challenge would be that we have already lived our life, whatever it was whether good or bad. Whether you were satisfied with your life or not? Your concern about your children could be understood. Now it is the life of your children which they want to live their own way. You want to live their life according to your experiences and means. It is going to be the real conflict in individual happiness. This would not do particularly in modern generations. This is no way that you are imposing your life on your children. It is their life and freedom which they would like to live. Please see that they are not denied from their life to live with. Yes...!!! It is agreed that you should be worried about them. Your concern for them that they do not go to any wrongful path is quite genuine.

When you started your life and when your children started their life, there is a difference of about three to four decades. The social, educational, economic and technical situations of your times are left much behind then the present existing ones. You would agree to this fact well. Possibly the struggle of your life survival in your times too would not have been that much comprehensive the way it appears to be today. You would not have faced then the kind of deviation the children are facing today. Morality has been strength of any society and this is going to be morale booster for your children too. Where morality conditions in any society are showing diminishing patterns and there is degradation of moral values then such society is bound to collapse in due course of time. We should not live in any confusion. Already our families are the smallest units of society but we cannot imagine our family having any independent existence keeping away from society. Every society has its own kind of views. Human civilizations are not able to root out the vices prevalent in society. Our only concern has been that as to how to protect our children from the vices existing in the society and to ensure to inculcate in them the moral values. There could be no doubt about it that your children should get benefit of your worldly experiences as and when they happen to be in earnest need of it. It is you only who has to do maximum worry about their children first then come the society.

What you wanted to be in your life? Whether you could or could not, this you would know better. But whatever you are today you should be satisfied with it. You must be approaching either in third or last innings of your life. But you should not think that your time is gone otherwise your dissatisfaction would leave adverse impact over your children. It would not be good for their future progressive improvement. Let the children live their life according to their own environment. It would be your duty to keep a sharp eye over their activities. Your moral values would make them strong. You would need not to make them learn. But they are children after all. They are innocent hearted. They may have tendencies to deviate for the reasons of their innocence. The support of your constructive and rich life experiences have the potential to take them beyond that destination where you wanted them to be. Effort should be that we should not start living life of our children but we should see our image in the life of our children. It is as simple that those who do efforts there are higher chances of committing mistakes. Those who do nothing for them there are no chances of mistake but they would not be able to do anything in their life.

Let your children commit errors. Then only they would be in a position to learn from their mistakes and rectify them for better achievements. When they are given freedom to identify their mistakes and work upon them to not to repeat again they prove to be better learners. The learning they are going to get this way would not only help them in their confidence building but would make them also full with practical life experiences. They would start feeling their life a bunch of joy and happiness. Do not let them arise any such occasion that they keep committing mistakes but make them understand what is good for them. While they commit mistakes with no elderly support around would be the situation when they are prone to go deep under depressed. Make them feel that you are around them to support of your experience. After realizing their mistakes your children become positively responsive to live a meaningful life. Let them realize that you never imposed your life to them but for their betterment. This feel among them would give a definite positive direction to live with. They would become emotionally linked with you. My emphasis for children would be that on occasions they would need to sacrifice their freedom and way of living since every parent lives and dies for the sake of their children. Parents are the real Gods on this earth. They would not be able to live life if their children are not happy. The youngsters should buy prosperity for parents it would make them to live their life too full of pleasure and happiness.

"Your concern about your children could be understood. Now it is the life of your children which they want to live their own way. You want to live their life according to your experiences and means. It is going to be the real conflict in individual happiness. This would not do particularly in modern generations. This is no way that you are imposing your life on your children. It is their life and freedom which they would like to live."

33

GIVING GRACIOUSLY

Every individual has hidden spiritual pleasure if he is able to discover it from within. The moment he attained that stage and has discovered it, he rises above the sensory pleasures. Our ancient philosophers have discovered that it is in fact very difficult for individuals to control their senses. So they remained in continuous search for evolving such practical methods with the help of which they could be in a position to induce a kind of psychological feeling in their mind which bestows them with spiritual pleasure. Because a perception always keeps reminding them that spiritual pleasure is always hidden within every individual. It is now for the individual only to look for the methods to discover it. If the individual is successfully able to achieve it then it would be the highest attainment of his life for which he has got birth on this earth.

The philosophers evolved that giving graciously is one of the most significant practical methods to seek sensory pleasures. It is a kind of alms giving where an individual is willing to share his wealth with others who are actually in need of it. Sharing one's own hard earned wealth with others is virtually a difficult state of mind. Psychology of human civilizations reveals that people do not get ready to part with their wealth even in the name of alms giving. The logic is quite practical and simple as to why one should give away anything what he has earned?

But discoveries of our ancient philosophers disclose that sharing of wealth is the highest level of mental situation and requires purification of mind. It could be a long and sustained process to create a kind of feel within human psychology to share his wealth with others. This would be the ultimate stage beyond the sensory pleasures.

Giving graciously should be the objective of human life. But at the time of giving if one feels pity about the needy persons, this feel is going to diminish your spiritual attainment. Feeling about pity with others directly correlates with human ego. This ego inflates further with the passage of time and overwhelms the entire human mind in due course. One human being feeling pity about another human being is not good by any standard of spirituality. While giving graciously you should have a sensory feeling for the receiver that he afforded an opportunity that you could attain rare pleasure for your mind. Once human mind gets ready for giving graciously this is completely a purified state of mind. One should have the feel that by accepting, the receiver in fact obliges the giver. One starts seeing an image of God in the receiver then only comes the actual stage of spiritual pleasure. Once reached that stage the person is no longer to move around for the search of mental peace.

Apart from material property people possess intellectual property too. A person has intellectual property in the form of knowledge. What the knowledge a person earns is not a kind of property he has possessed all of a sudden. Nor is a kind of property he received through inheritance. A person can inherit property by material transfer. It would be very difficult for that person psychologically to come forward and give some graciously to others in need. Because whatever the property he got through inheritance he enjoyed it. Neither could he develop any capacity nor any expertise to earn property on his own. He is spending that property with no restrictions, now he himself is feeling unsafe. Why should he give any part of it to others, would come to his mind? It is not essential components that people who earn knowledge would necessarily be in a position to earn money as well. But exceptions are also there. Like Steve Jobs, Bill Gates etc. Their knowledge of computer technology has made them richest person on this earth. It is their greatness that whatever money they earned by means of their technical knowledge they are using part of it in social welfare work for needy poor masses who are sick, suffering from malnutrition, children who are deprived of education, scarcity of medicines for better health and to fight their poverty conditions. For all this they felt their obligation to invest and donate a part of their money so earned by them. This would be a kind of spiritualistic pleasure for them which only they can experience and enjoy with. They understand that such a rare pleasure they could not have gained at any cost on the strength of their money.

Teaching communities earn knowledge in society. Intellectually equipped classes are in their best graceful positions to donate strength of their knowledge to the youth of today. The history of our civilizations has been evidence to this very fact that teacher's knowledge giving has produced better minds with constructive directions to our society. A knowledgeable person would have to ensure that moral values are established in our society which gives permanent strength to our coming generations. When a teacher gives education to his students then he should not forget that he is addressing and passing on his best teachings to generations. Caretakers of modern societies feel that there has been gross degradation of moral values and it so continues to be. Who can better understand this then a teacher, a thinker? Others would either be not in a position to understand it or if they would understand it, they would be doing politics with it. Social degradation would possibly be quite favorable situation in a degraded political environment. There would be no feel like giving graciously of moral values even. Teachers should not give only bookish knowledge to our children but they need to come forward graciously to give worldly knowledge too. In addition to their school examinations our students would have to pass through several tests in their coming challenging life, variety of tests for the sake of their society and towards their nation too. Why should they attempt to escape from such life tests? In adverse situations their bookish knowledge would not be in position to help. Did our teachers make them that capable? Our students would now be out to change the society. They would think and worry about their nation and it's not so good progress. Such knowledge would be of no use which could not help for a better society and the nation. Could our teachers give their knowledge graciously to next generations? Had it been that honestly then our society would not have been sufferer. Our teachers are in a position to give well intentioned positive direction to our society. Why then degradation of moral values in the society? Teachers would not be able to escape from their answerability. Teachers need to look into their inner self. They should go deep to their heart and think whether they could do all that for their society what they were expected to do? Answer is that they could not do that as continued degradation of social values are evident to that effect. There is a stage to be up to expectations. Teachers are capable enough to create such stages. They have opportunities amidst vast student community eager to learn from the teachers and further eager to go on doing something best for their society and the nation.

Educating graciously is incomparable. By giving knowledge to others graciously it always increases and never diminishes. Let our teachers feel realize the rare spiritual pleasure arising out of educating our youth. They would prove to be the future assets in our society. But the condition would be that the teacher should perform this task quite honestly and with a gracious mind. Incidentally the nature of intellectual property is like that you have to share it with others. That is different that the professionals charge price for sharing their intellectual property with others. This could well be influenced by existing materialistic cultures. Those who are not only true intellectuals but thinkers as well towards well being of the society and future of their youth they could never be professionals. They are not going to sell their intellect but they would give it to the needy one very graciously. They would not accept anything in return to it. Since their spirituality is their biggest strength which they would never like to lose under any circumstances. Possibly they have dedicated their complete life in search of such rare pleasure linked with graciously giving.

"Giving graciously should be the objective of human life. But at the time of giving if one feels pity about the needy persons, this feel is going to diminish your spiritual attainment. Feeling about pity with others directly correlates with human ego. This ego inflates further with passage of time and overwhelms the entire human body and mind in due course. While giving graciously you should have a sensory feeling for the receiver that he afforded an opportunity that you could attain the real pleasure for your mind."

34

RECREATE YOURSELF

When you take birth on this earth, can you say that you were all conscious about it? You were aware that you are born. Can you…??? You were born out of your mother's womb. You were not conscious at all. You did not make it happen. It was the nature which made it happen. Nature did it for you. You were not conscious when you were born. Even when you were infant you never knew what is all happening around you? When you were born you were the creation of the nature. During your childhood even you were quite innocent to your surroundings. But your innocence was being spoiled by the people in the outside world. It was happening against the law of nature which had never been within your control then. Biologically it is the systematic development of your mind which gradually takes you to a stage of self-conscious. Legally speaking below the seven years of age a child is considered to be completely innocent for the reasons that because of his lesser development of mind he is incapable to understand the nature of the act he is doing or that what is happening around him.

He does, he acts, he laughs, and he speaks unconsciously. He is made to learn to speak or to do the things. He follows and imitates what he is made to learn by his elders. He does all that unconsciously without knowing it whether it was good or bad. The issue to think upon before us is that while a child is passing through a phase of learning unconsciously for years altogether without properly understanding whether what could be either right or wrong? There is every possibility that children are exposed to such situations or practices which may corrupt their unconscious mind. Where such a spoiling environment persists then our children may be deviated to some wrongful path. Please do not blame the children. Whether they develop to be good or bad they ultimately reflect into their behavior the mindset of their elderly surroundings.

What does one intend about to create and then recreate himself? Are you capable enough to create and recreate yourself? Do you think so? Creation goes by the law of nature. The nature protects and grooms its creations. Such grooming has been subject to the conditions that we allow ourselves to the rule of nature. Neither we are in touch with the rule of nature nor are we allowing our children to be close to the nature. Therefore, the creation of the nature not following the rules remains unprotected. What the nature can do? Nature is helpless. When our children are put in unnatural environments then their childhood is spoiled. Their unbiased innocence has been corrupted. Anybody full with negative orientations can come in contact with them, spoil them and go away. This way their innocence has been taken away. Undoubtedly, it is very difficult for all of us to keep protecting our children from such adverse situations already prevalent in the society for the reasons of spoiled society mix ups. We are observing it minutely that today our children are behaving abnormally. Their innocence has gone very cleverly. They appear to be quite tense today for the reasons that they have lost their innocence in their childhood itself. This loss of their innocence is due to not so healthy external factors which the children are facing around. Once they continue with this tense frame of mind set as beautiful creations of nature they are lost.

Now what do we mean by recreation? Re-create yourself means to regain the innocence lost. Is the child now is capable enough to recreate himself once his innocence stands corrupted by negative surroundings? No. He is not because he is under the influence of external forces which are responsible for damaging his innocence. Then how to remove the influence of external forces from the mind of a developing child who is getting young day by day? One day he would be mature. Such influences would now be in the process of permanently setting down deep in the mind of the young boy or the girl. Does recreating himself means that the youth has to reborn? Physically not but spiritually yes. When our youth are in a position to remove those influences which have polluted their mind they would be in a position to free them from worldly negativities and would feel them to be completely reborn. What do you feel about that what you are? Do you find yourself in a position to understand you? You think about you. What others make you to think about you? How do you assess about self? Did you ever try to talk with your own self? I think very rarely? Have you ever felt about the content of 'I' or 'me' in your life? This 'I' is the input which has been given to you by the worldly forces that corrupted your innocence right since your birth and developing childhood. You are carrying it since then throughout your youth. Throw away the feel of 'I' from within 'you' and recreate yourself. You are reborn in your life time. This rebirth is quite conscious in the sense that you are completely aware about your innocence now. As compared to your infant and childhood innocence when you were unaware, now when you have become conscious about you, nobody can dare to take away your innocence. Your awareness about you is now full with enlightenment within you. Once you are self aware the worldly forces cannot spoil or corrupt your mind. You will live and enjoy your life the way you like it. People around you would also be benefitted by the vibrations of positive energy emanated from your enlightened personality.

By doing away with the feeling of 'me' one is able to establish complete control over him. Other way round he is not being controlled by others the way maliciously they intend to. This conscious control of one's 'own self' enables one to make fair, rightful and judicious decisions for his better and balanced life. Others would now not be in a position to dictate or influence your decisions. Your conscious awareness about your decision making would prove to be right. Mistakes in good faith are protected and made excusable under the law texts. Law considers a child who is above seven years of age and up to twelve years has developed sufficient levels of maturity of understanding biologically. Though the law protects such children from any legal liability but considers them to be sensitive enough to be corrupted by anyone with a negative orientation. In fact these are the young minds that are much sensitive and exposed to fast learning specifically negative ones and need more protection from such exposures.

Where one talk about recreating yourself by means of taking rebirth then it does not mean that the person would have to die, to reborn again. If in this life span only the person is able to gain victory over his feel of 'myself' it amounts to that he is reborn. He will remain aware despite being completely innocent. He will completely enjoy his birth to recreate him time and again. Nobody can take away you from your changed state of mind. Because in recreated state of your innocence there would be no situation of any conflict with your 'I' and simultaneously your awareness would make your consciousness further strong. Your sustained consciousness would pave your way for enlightenment. The purpose of human life ultimately is the peace of mind, happiness and that the man can do in the life in a better manner up to his capacity and satisfaction. A man himself should think of peace despite negative forces are at work. A person who is born again by throwing away his negativities and by orienting him positive is going to be boon for earthly maintenance of peace and let others also to live with peace. By his rebirth and recreations he would be a completely changed man to be helpful in creating such a favorable environment for happiness to prevail for all. The moment a man would get the enlightenment of his consciousness then the light of his knowledge would not be limited within the identified boundaries of a social system. It would brighten several civilizations from bad to good and good to better one. When you recreated yourself by taking 'you' out of 'I' then only it became certain that the external negativities would not be in a position to affect your consciousness. The positive energy of your 'rebirth' moving around you would make others feel the peace and the happiness. Yes...!!! Recreate yourself rebirth is possible in your life time.

"Have you ever felt about the content of 'I' or 'me' in your life? This 'I' is the input which has been given to you by the worldly forces that corrupted your innocence right since your birth and developing childhood. You are carrying it since then throughout your youth. Throw away the feel of 'I' from within 'you' and recreate yourself. You are reborn in your life time."

35

CHOOSING THE RIGHT PATH

Our life is a long unending journey and it continues even after your life time. Efforts are needed to be made this journey to be fruitful at the same time otherwise this beautiful journey would prove to be a simple waste. A journey going to be a waste would be a journey done without any purpose. Are we living on this earth for no purpose? Do we make assessment of our deeds on regular basis? As to what we gained? What we lost? Did we choose the right path to perform our life's journey? Did we complete the journey gainfully? Or we did that wastefully? What we did was in service of the mankind? Thus choosing the right path is an essential component in every one's life journey. Now the question would be that who will show you the right path? Is it necessary that some spiritual leader would teach you the right path? Can't you self-realize yourself and make search for right path? There is no doubt about it that relationship between a teacher and his disciple has been very pious and based upon emotional relationship. Searching for a real teacher has been a difficult task for anyone who in fact seriously looks for it. But once he is in a position to get the real teacher and has been able to follow his teachings then he should be confident enough that he is on to a right path.

The ultimate purpose of your life has been to reach close to the blessings of the Almighty Nature. If you feel that you are on to that path then you become certain about it that you are not going to pass away your life in a wasteful manner for no purpose. A human being becomes a real teacher after he passes through a lot of sufferings in his life. These sufferings may be given to him by the society itself may be related to his profession or otherwise. But there is always a spiritual touch for that man behind all these sufferings. The spiritual factor makes him to pass through the sufferings making him the real teacher. Your search then would be over because he is the one who would put you on to the right path. Such teachers are not the ordinary teachers but they are ordained with nature's blessings sent on this earth to help out the needy individuals. They are the vehicles of spiritual intellectuality with their body, speech, mind and their personality itself as a moving institution. The Almighty is the ultimate invisible force on this earth controlling and regulating the entire nature around us. The Almighty chooses such teachers and uses them as a medium for the purpose of spreading spiritual intellectuality for prosperity of the people. It would be up to us whether we have developed such ability within ourselves to get the blessings of such real teachers. Because the teacher only would show you the path what is right for you depending upon your attitude and the way of your thinking. It would not be necessary that the teacher would also move along the same path. You may have to move alone on to it. But once you are on the right path you would certainly reach up to ultimate destination of your mental peace and happiness not only for people at large as well.

Have you ever thought of the destination of your life's journey? Do you want to be rich? You want to be knowledgeable or an intellectual. Or you want to be spiritual either? We come across a number of religious paths prevalent on this earth. All these religions have their own paths and their varied kind of religious opinions. Off course on one point they are unanimous that they claim to show the path of salvation to their followers. The exponents of such religions from time to time are the agents of salvation representing the Almighty. There are thousands and thousands of followers moving on the path shown by the respective religions considered to be the right path. Despite that there is lack of peace and happiness on this earth. The question is why? Whether the teachings of different religions are failing in to get up to the right path? Or else the followers of such beliefs could not rise up to the expectations and teachings of such religions. This could be a major factor behind what we are coming across large scale poverty conditions amongst people, problems relating to human health, lack of prosperity and religion based strategic tension across the boundaries of different nations.

Where religious salvations are the right paths to those who are well off does it include also the poor, uneducated, people dying of hunger and suffering from ill heath? They do not know about the A, B, and C of any religious belief while struggling day and night for their mere survival, their family members and the kids on this earth. Majority of people are deprived off basic minimum necessities for them as human beings. The basic question would be that who would show these people of their rightful path? Where is the path which shows them and the kids to earn bread to eat? They never wish their bread to be with butter. Simply that path which earns them bread with same salt sprinkled over it. An empty stomach would never enjoy any religious music let it be even sweat one. It is certain then majority of people would never be able to see and know their right path in life. One day they would die struggling in starvation. Their children would also follow the same 'path' born to die ultimately. Not born to live. This social and economical inequality prevalent in our society discourages one to the core of his heart. This makes one to make a complaint with the Almighty, as to why this imbalance, this inequality and for what purpose? Oh…!!! The Almighty, could you please see this gross injustice on this earth? Who are the agents of such injustice? Can't you punish them the Almighty? How are you able to watch and bear the miseries of this majority of people? Who would show them the right path of health, prosperity and justice? Or else you would leave them at the mercy of the agents of such beliefs.

So choosing the right path for every human being on this earth would prove to be a myth. The agents of paths of salvation also play picks and choose. In a given socio-economic conditions of society, although every person is born equal on this earth, there are varying scales of equality. There is no equality among unequal while the natural fact is that all are born equal. When the born equals became unequal would be a point to ponder with. Who made them unequal after they are born equal? When examined putting on the scales of practicality such concepts prove painfully contradictory. It would be humbly suggested that unless the states come forward with welfare oriented positive initiatives with all honest intentions to help this majority people in struggles of their survival they would have no occasion to think even the path which could be right or wrong for them. What to talk about their salvation? They are just living on this earth to die one day. That's it.

"The agents of paths of salvation also play picks and choose. In a given socio-economic conditions of society, although every person is born equal on this earth, there are varying scales of equality. There is no equality among unequal while the natural fact is that all are born equal. When the born equals became unequal would be a point to ponder with."

36

LACK OF SELF-CONFIDENCE

Superstitions have been much prevalent in our existing societies. We do not ever try to examine scientific considerations behind such superstitions. People look for favorable stars and keep waiting for things to happen. What could be the thinking behind that? Whether it could be scientifically proved that the things would exactly happen the way one visualizes subject to the conditions that the stars favor? Can't individuals make things happen the way they like by putting in their sincere efforts despite the fact that stars were not in favor? Yes…!!! It is the firm determination and the will power of a man which makes things happen despite all odds. Those who wait for things to happen subject to favor of stars they are on to big mistake. Without putting in honest efforts and hard work even your luck is also not going to do any favor to you. Whether you want a peaceful mind or a disturbed mind? You wish to have joy in your life or miseries. Who is your God or who is the devil? It is all created by you. Never live your life as per chance or under the influence of superstitions. If luck would have been particular thing would happen for me otherwise not. Such state of your mind would fill you up with a sense of fear and anxiety.

This looks to be more scientifically convincing when you live by your working capability things are bound to happen in accordance with your efforts you have put in. Moreover, you would be in complete control of what is happening to your efforts. Human scientific temper has been based upon reasoning and well calculated logical thoughts. There is a need to understand behind superstitions catching our mind. We start depending upon superstitions because we fail to create any internal or external environment within ourselves for happening of things in a right manner. Without making any effort in a right direction we start looking for favorable stars to make things happen for us. Make it a point that it is not stars but it is your well designed effort and minutely coordinated thinking process within yourself would definitely make the things happen for you. Yes…!!! You will start experiencing with passage of time that happening of events in life are proportionately dependent upon your intelligent manipulation of existing situations to make your life worth living and full of joy.

May be there is a popular feeling that the superstitions have scientific basis. They become deep built in with our cultural sensibility. Modern scientific research does not reveal any link with existing superstitions which could put them within the parameters of scientific temper. Scientific temper goes for the reason, logic and the truth of existing verifiable facts. Let us not be ignorant and too innocent. We should apply our logical mind, search for the reason and the truth then act upon it. That only would be the secret behind well being in our life. Meaning of truth is having some facts of life which are in existence which one can examine him. Lord Buddha said in very express terms that for a logical person there should be no reason to act upon by getting completely blind following superstitious beliefs. If 'I' said something to 'you' or attempted to make 'you' understand certain facts, then why should 'you' believe it to be true, what 'I' said? Because 'I' said it, so it is true that is why 'you' are following it. No…!!! Instead of blindly believing the statement to be true, you examine its truth with the help of your knowledge. Then believe it when you find it to be true. Truth of certain facts is also dependent upon existing situation and circumstances. It may not be necessary that what one said would be exactly the same in different situations as well. This may vary from one place to other and from one situation to other. You need to have faith for such things only which are duly examined by your logical mind and that found to be right thing by you.

How would we get logic? Why do we become superstitious? Whether the reason behind our superstitions is lack of confidence within us? Whether we ever thought of it as to how come we got this lack of confidence? Is some kind of fear has been made to set in our mind? Who are the carriers of this fear? Psychological researches reveal that the moment our mind grips in with superstitious fear, it stops thinking. There is no room of any logic for a mind full with fear. Under the circumstances of superstition our society has its own in built fear factors. Where our mind has been left not even worth to think cautiously and made blind. This is institutional demerit of our social system. Our education system has been made so weak that youth are not being properly educated. There is no need to be emphasized that education strengthens the logical capacity of a person. And such education we are not getting. It amounts to mental handicap where people are either uneducated or even educated that too insufficiently. People with mental handicap would be quite dangerous situation for their will power. Where lack of education is at large then mental handicap is bound to be there. The individuals would be lacking in confidence that is certain and would be more sensitive falling prey to superstitious beliefs very easily. When human mind has been under fear influenced by the carriers of superstitions then how come it would have the needed will power? Under such circumstances it would become tendency of getting blind for superstitious faith depending more on some miracles to happen rather than any efforts made for getting things done in right direction. Such blind tendencies in superstitious escalates further.

Could we see the position of planets and stars within the frame work of scientific parameters? No doubt…!!! It is scientific. Is the position of planets and stars has to do something with the happenings in human life? Whether stars influence the thinking process of human mind superstitiously? Often we hear people saying that their stars are not good. They are failing in and not getting success. Their health is not good following bad stars. No progress in their work. They keep getting loss in business till the planets are made to cool down. People think, let stars are favorable then some pious work would be started. Now what to say about the thinking of people? If they are not putting in hard work make sure stars are not going to help anyway. Man with no other resources would get close to starvation troubles and serious health hazards. Do not blame the stars for your troubles that they are not good. You are inviting your troubles by sitting idle doing nothing and waiting superstitiously for your star to do favor. You have to work out your problems so as to make your stars in your favor. If education is not proper then human minds would not be powerful to address to their problems effectively and get more easy leanings towards superstitious practices. Then how could they do life's struggle. In this competitive world they would be defeated. Youth are not going to get jobs remaining unemployed where stars would not be able to help them out. Our social system need to be put on the right tract by its caretakers. Our people are required to be properly trained by our social institutions to be more based on logic with scientific temper rather than follow superstitious beliefs. Drawbacks in the system are the results of the bad policies adopted by the system managers. Bad social policies devoid of science would not only make the system weak but would also reduce the self confidence level in comprehensive thinking of our youth. Planets or stars are neither in your favor nor against you. They would be there standing by your side provided the acts done by you are up to the level adequate enough to make your life successful. When seen honestly your acts were not up to the level then you should not expect success. Stars are not going to work for you. Do not look for excuses for your life failures by blaming your stars. By all this you only are going to be the looser. Do you seek excuses to impress upon others and to conceal your drawbacks in the eyes of others? But the drawbacks would so remain there. Better you should work upon and remove your drawbacks instead. This only reflects the level of lack of self-confidence in you. Forget the planets and stars. Start making your honest efforts. When you are right, keeping your self-confidence intact then there is no reason that your planets and stars are going to create any difficulties for you.

They would be most out to favor you because you believe in you. Learn to trust yourself.

"Do not blame the stars for your troubles that they are not good. You are inviting your troubles by sitting idle doing nothing and waiting superstitiously for your stars to do favor. You have to work out your problems so as to make your stars in your favor. If education is not proper then human minds would not be powerful to address to their problems effectively and get more easy leanings towards superstitious practices."

———————————————

37

STRESS MAKES YOU STRONG

It is often said that living under stress is harmful. Stress causes mental injury due to excessive blood pressure ultimately risking for a heart disease. Do you ever feel that what are the causative factors behind your mental and physical stress? Today's world has become very fast for no specific reason. Sometimes we feel that we keep running throughout the day only to get badly tired by the evening. It would be a totally different issue to link fastness of our life with fast socio-economic development of any society or any nation. Where our daily run is not focused, by the evening it seems to be wastage of all efforts giving rise to your nights stressful. Again the same run starts by the next morning only to get full with stress by the night. It happens and is very common not only in under developed or developing societies but even in the societies which could be said to be fairly developed.

Stress to a person could be of society induced or economic stress due to unemployment or loss in business. Family related stresses are now-a-days very common due to unnecessary misunderstanding among the members of the family. Where people are sensitive to the cause of their nation building, they seem to be more worried about the political scenario of their country. They come under stress when they watch the politically rival groups fighting each other due to their opposite political ideologies proving detrimental to the interest of the nation. You cannot prevent yourself from getting under stress otherwise you are person absolutely senseless. How to get rid of such day to day stress in your life? No such question arises. You cannot get rid of them at all. The only way out is to get you ready to face them head on.

Why do not you use this stress to your advantage? You must be surprised. You would be thinking that how come your stress is going to be of any advantage to you? But be normal. Yes…!!! It is possible. You can convert your stress to your advantage. The way getting under stress is a natural phenomenon for individuals, in the same manner using stress to your advantage is also quite natural. You spend time and money in managing your stress with the help of medicine and other therapies. It is only suppressed under the influence of medicines and it can flare up any moment once the influence of medicines diminishes. At the same time it is harmful to the body system also. So why not to look for such psychological possibilities to use the stress to your advantage? Human mind has a very strong working capacity. Your stress is nothing but is a kind of your mind set which has been put in a situation of receiving negative stimulus so it is responding accordingly in the form of stress to you. Can you put yourself away from such negative stimulus? Why not? Yes…!!! You can. It only needs a shift in your mindset from negative impulses to positive impulses. This shift you can make happen since you only are encountering with such stresses in the given circumstances.

It is possible for you to master your circumstances. Then why to let the stress come to you at all? If you are looking to your stress with negative orientation then it is definitely going to harm you. Try to see your stress with a positive orientation. It may be difficult but it is possible for making a shift in your mindset. Try to feel your mental stress. You are under stress for a reason. You are in a better position to identify the reasons causing stress for you. Work out if you are in a position to remove the reasons or the factors causing stress to you. There is every possibility that you would succeed to find solutions to your stress problems. Sit with a positive mindset that every problem has its own solutions provided you are looking for solutions with a positive approach. The moment you happen to shift your mind that you can solve and remove your problem you start experiencing strong from within your body. A strong and focused mind only can solve the problems peacefully. A mind under stress is disturbed mind lacks in to focus the problem.

Use your stress as a motivator for you to strengthen you from within so that you are able to remove the reason which is causing stress to you. Stress could in fact be good for you since it creates a fighting capacity within you provided you are determined to fight it out. You may have certain goals in your life to accomplish with but you come under the pressure of stress. It may sound strange to you but it is true that your stress is going to be a motivator for you when you become determined to take action pursuant to your goal. You come under stress easily because you are sensitive towards your life targets. This in fact is very good being sensitive towards goals. Those who are not they may be least bothered. Stress phase in your life comes temporarily to make you strong and it goes away. Believe me, your stress would push you and accelerate your activities by acting as a tool. You come under stress in your life, it is essential for you. A regular dose of stress in small quantities would help you in developing resistance power and make your body and mind capable enough to face future stresses. Once your mind develops adaptability towards stresses and at the sometime accelerates your fighting capacity from within, physically and mentally, then you find yourself in a position to be a good action taker and sharp decision maker at the same time.

How come this all becomes possible? Yes…!!! It is all scientific. Researches reveal that in the moments of acute stress newer nerve cells are generated in your brain. These newer nerve cells biologically improve the performance of your mind. This you will perceive in the form of enhanced focusing capacity of your mind, increased levels of concentration, better feel of your memory and learning capacity. This state of shift of mind you would attain through a regular but rigorous practice. This is not going to happen overnight. Through perseverance one day you would be able to achieve such a mindset which is ready to counter any stressful situation in your life and ready to convert that stress to your advantage. You would then yourself feel that you are ready to welcome stress and make this stress work for you.

Please add meaning to your life instead of spoiling your life in stressful conditions. Stress is for you, whether lesser in quantity or more in quantity. You cannot avoid stress while living in worldly conditions. Now when it is certain that you have to live amidst stressful conditions then better to build such resilience to counter with it and use it to your advantage. Countering with your stress would be dependent upon the fact whether how you view this stress for you? If you find that the stress affects you in a more harmful manner then you are expected to react more sharply. You need to retrain your brain in stressful conditions and even after that. Problem arises only when you are full with negative thoughts that stress has overpowered you in its grips. You seem to have no way to counter it out. You are scared that stress would damage your life. Make it a point that this negative thinking process in you would weaken you from within and making you lose the battle against stress. Once stress creeps in your mind it settles down there for a longer duration provided you surrender and do not resist timely. You start feeling within yourself that stress is setting down, welcome it and start retraining your mind. Your trained mind would make your stress as a helping tool. You will feel that you are able to make the stress work for you, getting you the needed strength to be the winner.

Try to realize in your life that difficult journey of life becomes easier and pleasant once you link them with a purpose and definite goal to achieve with. Purpose of your life motivates you if you are serious about it. Stress in your life is an essential natural condition. By stressing your mind you have learnt to give positive indicators to your stress. You have given a purpose to your stress. No doubt making your stress purposeful is not an easy task. It is difficult but it is possible. For making it possible the essential requirement is that your body and mind has to pass through all those difficulties, rigors and hardships otherwise it would not be possible. Stress would prove to be a good friend for you provided you have purposefully linked that with your life's journey and the definitive pious goal. Work upon it, I do have worked regularly, it works.

"Stress phase in your life comes temporarily to make you strong and it goes away. Believe me, your stress would push you and accelerate your activities by acting as a tool. You come under stress in your life, it is essential for you. A regular dose of stress in small quantities would help you in developing resistance power and make your body and mind capable enough to face your future stresses."

38

I AM NO BODY

You will reach up to a stage of thought process in your life that 'I am no body'. Your inner conscious time and again enquires about as to 'Who are you'? You have taken birth on this earth it should have some meaning. What could be the difference after all in your being some body or your being no body? If it appears to you that you are also something then what is wrong in it? Do you feel that it reflects your proud? Or else you have become so strongly spiritual that your being something even makes you feel that you are no body. That's great. Whether you have felt realized your feelings when you are thinking in objectivity? Or how do you feel when you start thinking around you subjectively? Try to feel the difference and experience the emotions with your closed eyes. You have your vast inner world within you. Go deeper into your inner world. That is subjective and private to you. You have your own emotions for yourself and also for the people around you. What is private to you nobody can enter into it. Your thinking process within you is essentially personal. This only you can visualize. Your thoughts coming out of this process have deep links with your inner world. This only ensures purity of your thoughts. This is unparallel. Where there is purity there is pleasure.

You would have watched authors, poets, scientists, researchers. Observe their daily routine from morning till evening or late night. You would find that they have no time to spare. You would not find them sitting in public unnecessarily chatting around and wasting their time. They have their own large inner world of creativity. They always look for privacy where they develop original ideas to pen down in the form of their writings. They become successful in bringing their consciousness close to their inner world. There are people like politicians who have to be among public, because of nature of their assignment. Their thoughts are for public good since they have to win elections. The question could be whether politicians have no private life of their own? They may have but for a politician in true sense his private life remains at the disposal of public at large. When he is in public he has got an identity and the moment he reaches home, he feels himself that he is no body. Without a gathering behind him a politician loses his face. Loss of face for a politician is quite painful because he is 'no body' in private.

An author or poet can claim against the public at large that he has his private life which is quite rich and full of happiness. The creativity he generates is for the welfare of the mankind for generations. That's the kind of asset he possesses which no body on this earth can take away from him. This is subjective, which he only understands and enjoys for that such thoughts belong to him. Thinkers do possess creativity through their writings. Their thinking process continues in prolonged isolations when they keep themselves absolutely cut off from the rest of the world. Their isolation is productive and full with creative ideas for betterment of coming generations on this earth. Can we say that they are living their private life, the way they liked it? Are they content to themselves? But they keep thinking about their fellow human beings and their betterment, even when they are supposed to be subjective. They keep worrying about others, about their depravity. As to why they have sufferings in their life? As to why majority of people on this earth are deprived off even from their basic minimum needs of their day to day life? Why the world leadership overlooks their miseries? These people lead their life worst than animals. Why do not resourceful leaders come forward to help them out? Authors, thinkers, philosophers have their vast inner world where they remain busy in searching for ways and means to address to the miseries of people in the outer world.

They understand that they are 'no body' but still through their writings and concerns they would keep suggesting to the system mangers to minimize miseries of people on this earth.

Yes...!!! I am no body. I have no life of my own. If I am able to earn my bread that is sufficient for my minimum requirements. I am not content within myself. I am forced by my sensitivities to think about other human beings too who are not able to earn their bread even and go starving. Not because that they do not want to work to earn but because they have no work to earn. This in fact is a system fault which failed in generating sufficient work making them to go without work. Tomorrow they would go weak following starvations. It would make them incapable physically and mentally to be not able to do work perfectly and later to be blamed as worthless. It becomes very painful to say as to who is to be blamed? Why not the system instead? The result is that they are the worst sufferers of this blame game. Any system, it has been noticed, never concedes to its faults. An author thinks about them and their problems objectively but in a subjective manner. I have my public life, thinking about people and their miseries day and night and raise their voices through my writings. I know that it would be very difficult for the system to digest what I communicate through my writings. My writings could be unbiased and bitter eye openers. It would be more suggestive, improving upon rather any criticism. But it is also true at the same time that sooner or later the ice has to melt down. Whatever the kind of system managers could be they would not be able to turn deaf for all the times. I know that me despite being 'no body', am still hopeful that one day the system would learn this bitter truth that it is not going to have its perpetual existence of its own without the supportive strength of its people.

Living in private means living close to spirituality, is not true always. Why do not take people also close to the doors of divinity by allowing them to participate with your privacy? May be your peace of mind is disturbed making hurdles to your journey to be spiritual. It could be one mind set. The other mind set could be quite different to it. Your public life which has been dedicated to the cause of people also leads you to the path of spirituality. The public life brings essential forces from outside and injects in you deep inside. Who says that public life necessarily calls for you to be a leader? The actual satisfaction of your life and the spiritual pleasure would not be in the sense to be a leader but it would be your sensitivity and the concern for the people at large for their betterment that the voice you raised for them through your writings would make you feel great in yourself. That goes subjective pleasure for you but by objective means. You would see that you forced the system by your writings to be proactive for the people who are deprived off their basic minimum needs. The stony ice was made to break for the majority under privileged to establish this fact that you are 'some body'.

"I am not content within myself. I am forced by my sensitivities to think about other human beings too who are not able to earn their bread even and go starving. Not because that they do not want to work to earn but because they have no work to earn. This in fact is a system fault which failed in generating sufficient work making them to go without work."

39

SUPREME CONSCIOUSNESS

Simply taking birth passing away life somehow and then leave this world is similar to what the animals do. We are human beings and not animals but we are not conscious as human beings if we just live our life and pass away. No doubt...!!! We are conscious about our family, near and dear ones. We are worried about their livelihood, they should be cared and brought up in a better manner, be properly educated for their future career. Our consciousness is self-centered. We do not bother to know what is happening to our just next door unless it is likely to harm us anyway. If it some way appears to affect us adversely then we react otherwise we keep silent. Do we know what all is happening in our society is not well? There are crimes happening in society and state machinery is failing to control with. Women in society are molested and raped. Victims are our fellow human beings. Culprits are from amongst us only. You may escape your responsibility contending that it's state's function to stop crimes. You are right but this also is equally correct that you only have conferred this authority to state to firmly act upon. Then how can you escape from your ultimate responsibility by making any such vague statement and keeping yourself completely unaware about it?

Let us not talk consciousness or supreme consciousness in its psychological or spiritual sense. You are working on attaining supreme consciousness for years and years altogether sitting in dense forests or in caves and mountains. By practicing for years in isolation you now claim that you are able to know yourself. You have acquired abundant knowledge through all these years. So you are now conscious, you feel. But how does your consciousness is going to benefit the mankind as you said that you practiced it in isolation? While in isolation you were for away from society. If the society needs to be benefitted by your attainment then the important requirement is that you come down to live in the society. No doubt, you have reached to a point of self-realization. But you cannot be so self-centered. May be you prefer to live in isolation now for the reasons that you have been accustomed to it. Living in crowd may distract you from your consciousness and disturb your peace of mind. Your real test of consciousness would be that despite living in worldly crowd you remain so content and undisturbed that you are able to lead this society out of its worries it has been put in.

There are worries in the society prevalent since the society came into being. Worries in the society are self created. This could be because of their lack of consciousness which they never attempted to attain for the sake of worldly pleasures. Worldly pleasures are for human beings but developing lust for such pleasures proves to be harmful. Enjoying pleasures by people has a deep relationship with human consciousness. Those who are able to win over their worries are able to attain their peace of mind. Sustained peace of mind is a precondition for a person to remain happy with joy. Being spiritual is nothing to do with any religious faith. You could be spiritual even without practicing any particular religion. Your spiritualistic approach is nothing but a state of your mind and the same would be directly proportional to your level of consciousness. Your supreme consciousness would be the ultimate level of your practicing mind. You want that peace make a permanent place in your mind. That would only be possible when you are able to ensure purity of thoughts to stay on in your mind. It would be the strength level of your consciousness which is going to be deciding factor whether your mind is going to be dominated by positive thoughts or negative thoughts? Now could you be expected to be with no thoughts? That is called 'zero' state of human mind. Zero state of your mind is possible even while leading a worldly life. Human mind does not go in absolute zero state. It needs deep consciousness to ensure about the zero state of your mind by consciously not allowing any thoughts to creep in your mind. You would be quite amazed to think of a mind without thoughts. Common thinking is that and it is true also, where there is 'human mind' thoughts have to be there, whether positive or negative ones depending upon individual mindset. Can you think of a mind full with thoughts but still it enjoys zero state of mind? Yes...!!! That is possible for a mind with 'supreme consciousness'.

Keeping in view the prevalent worries all across the globe, present day world is in desperate need of minds with consciousness if not supreme ones. The world needs minds with purity of thoughts capable to understand and appreciate human feelings and their emotions deep. Where people are out to unleash violence and causing injuries to one another then who is there to stop them? But why, after all, we fight at each other? Why to expect that police to come and stop us? Can't we ourselves live with peace giving no reason to the police to interfere with? To be self conscious where is the necessity for a man to go and live in forests and mountains? We should not hope that one day some saint full with 'supreme consciousness' from mountains would come and save us from all our worries? May be he is not able to live in this world with messy crowd. You would not be able to benefit yourself from his state of supreme consciousness. Make a determination with yourself that you are equally capable to attain consciousness of your mind even while living through your worldly life. You cannot escape from living in this world for the reasons that you have your own family and worldly obligations to fulfill with. You have to fulfill all these obligations at the same time to be conscious as well. You are conscious when you are doing what you are supposed to do while carrying your family obligations. You will be free from all worries specially generated by a mind polluted with negative thoughts. Problem arises when you do, what you are not supposed to do. You do not do, what you are supposed to do. This is your negative consciousness. You very well know that you are negative, doing consciously something wrong, but still you do it. Be sure, worries are bound to happen to you. You cannot escape from it because you only are the creator of your worries. Your conscious mind learns lessons from its mistakes done consciously or unconsciously. You become conscious to commit no wrongs, avoid worries and gradually you attain the state of 'supreme consciousness' by your virtues and positive mind. You are doing that only what you are supposed to do and what your conscious mind enjoys to do. No worries at all.

"You would be quite amazed to think of a mind without thoughts. Common thinking is that and it is true also, where there is 'human mind' thoughts have to be there, whether positive or negative ones depending upon individual mindset. Can you think of a mind full with thoughts but still it enjoys zero state of mind? Yes...!!! That is possible for a mind with 'supreme consciousness'."

40

THE LIGHT IN YOU

Whenever we see around our life with darkness we start making efforts to fight it out. There are well calculated phases of darkness in your life. It is exactly similar the way you witness your nights with darkness followed by day lights. Day comes and the night goes away. It is an essential natural process. I have heard people saying to fight out the dark. The way it is a natural process, same is the situation with we human beings. What could be the dark phases of your life? Off course the worries which are results of your worldly desires. Your worries make you feel painful when you are trapped by them. Nobody can trap you against your will unless you allow yourself to fall in their trap. That's the point. You allowed yourself to be full of worries. Now you want to get rid of your worries without making any change in your pursuit for desires. The dark phase of your life starts. Where is the need to fight with dark? Just lit a lamp the dark would go away. Do you hope that you can fight with dark without making an effort to light a lamp? You can't.

Lighting of a lamp would be applicable for purposes of removing physical darkness. That is an artificial method to remove physical darkness and would also depend upon resources available at our disposal. Where we are not able to create permanent resources to keep generating artificial light and in case resources are exhausted then the darkness is bound to prevail. The darkness has to go with the sun starts rising and the darkness has to be there the moment the sun starts setting down. This is the natural process wherein days and nights keep following up. Human beings, the flora and the fauna are so dependent on the phases of light and the darkness of the nature that even a minor deviation from it absolutely disturbs the entire physiology of these organisms. This natural process goes to show that phases of light and darkness are equally essential for the purposes of survival on this earth. My humble submission would be then where is the scope to fight out the darkness. It is by nature that darkness would follow the light. Without the phase of darkness you would not be able to enjoy the brightness of light. Then why to be scared of darkness after all? When darkness is so essential for our survival then why to have a feeling of contempt for darkness? That would be a very difficult question to reply for. To my opinion there should not be any question at all keeping in mind the fact that it is an essential natural process. How about a situation where there are days only and no nights? Would it be acceptable? No. Why…!!! You must be surprised how come it is going to be possible? Make it possible if you can. No. It is not possible. Then accept this true fact that you would have to pass through phases of darkness of the nights. Then why to feel about keeping at a distance from darkness? Live with it and enjoy it without any feel of contempt.

You are living in dark under a hope that the light has to come next then dark is not going to scare you anymore. Human life passes through many phases of darkness full with ups and downs in our life. You would not find a single person on this earth who has not suffered through dark phases in his life. It could be in the form of career failures, bodily and mental sufferings, feel of pains arising out of unfulfilled human desires. A human life is full with pains and pleasures. A single pain gives more sufferings than the amount of many pleasures. You might have realized it. Did you ever think about to reverse this situation? Can a single moment of pleasure is able to remove the pains arising out of number of sufferings? I think no. You cannot avoid painful darkness in your life but you can successfully reduce the number of sufferings with the help of the light within you. The human mind is very strong to convert the phases of sufferings of life into pleasant phases and to reduce the pain.

But the point is that we are unable to utilize our mind to its maximum potential. Your mind is the seat of knowledge which would strengthen you from within. Attainment of knowledge takes you up to the stage of enlightenment.

Your journey from darkness to light is a journey from ignorance to the stage of gaining knowledge. What does mean the knowledge for you? Knowledge is not a thing which could be gained all of a sudden. The knowledge is what you have acquired by yourself by developing capacity to understand. It generates light in you and has been due to your continuous and honest efforts made through perseverance. Your knowledge about you to know as to who are? With what objectives you are living your life on this earth? You want to develop knowledge about your fellow human beings. A knowledge that if you are not able to help fellow human beings then you are not going to harm them either. Knowledge ignites you from within to not to do any such an act which is unbecoming of you as a human being. May be you are literate and educated but this does not mean that you are knowledgeable too. Our history of human civilizations reveals that there have been people on this earth who were not educated but had acquired abundant knowledge and did welfare of the mankind. Process of gaining knowledge is to pass through a rigorous mental exercise for the purpose of understanding human behavior in relation to the nature and mutual human relationships. This universe is full of unlimited knowledge making you enlightened about your role to play on this earth. Basic varieties of knowledge are identified as social and scientific. If one is utilizing his knowledge to struggle in fighting out the human miseries he is an individual who has been enlightened from within and making in efforts to get this world rid off its darkness.

Knowledge must be all about to minimize the human miseries. You are responsible for the miseries you are suffering from. Knowledge would be of no use either to you or the society where you apply your knowledge to the detriment of society. The society is badly harmed by negativity. Your good knowledge only is the light within you which would protect you from the darkness of you negative thoughts. Do not expect that some other person would be able to light within you unless you make efforts and respond to it positively. A person who is enlightened with knowledge would show you the way only but the journey in search of light has to be completed by you only. Your life is precious and is abundant with knowledge. Once the light of your knowledge has come to stay permanently within you it is bound to enlighten not only you but also the people around you. You would make people realize this truth that they have mental capability to win over their miseries with the help of the light inside them.

"You cannot avoid painful darkness in your life but you can successfully reduce the number with the help of the light within you. The human mind is very strong to convert the phases of sufferings of life into pleasant phases and to reduce the pain. But the point is that we are unable to utilize our mind to its maximum potential."

41

YOU FEEL INSPIRED

There are occasions in your life when you feel that your life is full of achievements. You are content with this wonderful world. Whatever you achieved in your life that is not just all of a sudden. Your achievements are result of your rigorous and consistently honest efforts made by you for all the years. When you are thinking high your achievements also become of high level. Your achievements could be influenced by social considerations or materialistic considerations, but in the centre of all that you have the pious goal of human welfare to the best of your capacity. Do you ever feel to be self-inspired? You feel inspirations coming from inside you making you to boost your confidence. It happens just the reverse too. Despite your all sincere and honest efforts you fail to achieve the way you wanted. It happens. You would be all disappointed. Human disappointment is not the way of life. Human mind has to keep searching the ways and means to win over its disappointments. That's the only way out otherwise the human civilizations are to go in vain. No way, it is going to be seen as commendable thing.

Inspiration is a mindset which accelerates and activates you from within to perform yourself in a manner to achieve your targets they way you so wanted. Right from your childhood you are living in an environment which is full with positive inspirations for the reasons of your parents and the kind of family background you have. But every child is not fortunate to get an inspiring environment right from his childhood. Parental care is significant but all parents are not properly educated due to societal poverty conditions. They do have economic insecurity too. So they become incapable to inspire their children and ultimately such children are left uncared. In the long run they struggle for their survival fighting out their poverty conditions leaving behind any further possibility to get inspired due to lack of education. No doubt it is responsibility of the system to adopt serious measures to educate our children who are from the weaker sections and are worst affected by societal poverty conditions. But the system fails to inspire children who are deprived from childhood schooling and education despite the fact that the governments have statutory duty to ensure proper care and protection to such children. Hunger is the compelling factor that our children go in child labor leaving behind education. Our governments carelessly sit with their fingers crossed. Who to inspire them? How to inspire them? This becomes painful tragedy in existing societies that children are struggling in their childhood with no occasion for self-inspiration.

When you feel inspiring make it a point that you have started thinking beyond yourself. Now you are able to know that who are you and what are your limits? Thinking beyond you is really amazing. Does it mean a kind of thinking where one goes to think crossing over his own limits? Is it possible? Again a big question can a man has his limits to think and whether he could be confined within such limits? No...!!! Absolutely not. Gaining knowledge has no limits whatsoever. So would be your unlimited urge for awaking people by the knowledge so gained by you. Inspiration from within you awakens you to newer possibilities and enables you to travel beyond the human limits. It is awareness about you and making others aware about themselves. You were an ordinary man you so feel. But you felt elevated when you were not self centered and feeling concerned about welfare of others. You are self inspired to think as to why a group of human beings exploits another group of human beings in this world? This question is as old as has been human civilizations. The matter of surprise has been that such a sensitive question remains unanswered. There continues to be hatred and lack of brother hood among human beings. It is the politics of nations which is mainly responsible for prevailing situations of hatred. This needs to be done away with. But where is the initiative? This is bothering.

Feeling of self-inspiring should not be strictly individualistic. You felt inspired, you achieved. That is good. We at the same time have other fellow human being. They could not be self inspired for various reasons which are due to the social imbalances. They could not get their proper schooling and failed to get proper grooming. Now once, self inspired what could we do for their social and economic betterment? Without doubt, it is a difficult task. One can argue that in a welfare state it is the responsibility of the state to take necessary initiatives for betterment and advancement of their people. To educate them, groom them properly and make them self capable to face the social and economic struggles in their future life. That's the correct argument.

Make others also enjoy that inspiration is a sensational feeling of elevation not only from within but from outside as well. It ignites one for newer possibilities when we develop capacity to think beyond our limitation even. At the time of self-inspiration and also inspiring others, every single day is going to be significant for you. Every day would be just another day opening up opportunities full with challenging possibilities. Make yourself up to accept the challenges otherwise lost opportunities never come again. Once inspirations fail since you did not respond to, well in time to those opportunities, you get stressed and depressed. You need to realize this situation at this moment as to who is responsible for all that? You will feel a sudden loss of enthusiasm, excitement and energy within you. This will not be good for you. You have to see to stop this situation, else it would prove to be damaging for you in your life. The great thing for inspiration is that it is never driven by any lust or greed. The persons who are inspired are completely transformed and while motivating others they never expect any consideration for it. That's a kind of spiritual feel for them. Think beyond yourself. Work upon your mind. Go beyond this world you will achieve self actualization to inspire others. Feel the kind of stage in your life that no obstacle comes in your way and you move ahead with an infinite strength. Always fix a higher goal for yourself of seeing the mankind by inspiring them and making them sensitive, energetic, full of life peace and love. That would be an occasion for you to celebrate the achievements of your fellow human beings.

"Inspiration from within you awakens you to newer possibilities and enables you to travel beyond the human limits. It is awareness about you and making others aware about themselves. You were an ordinary man you so feel. But you felt elevated when you were not self centered and feeling concerned about welfare of others."

42

JUDGE YOURSELF HONESTLY

If you are a teacher then your students are the best judge. They judge you in a most impartial manner about your performance while you deliver lectures before them. A doctor is to be best judged by his patients. A business person is to be best judged by his customers. Where you wish to impartially judge someone, it would not be possible unless you stand apart from him. An honest judgment needs complete detachment about anything or any person. How can you impartially judge a thing which is owned by you? You cannot be impartial about a thing which you own. It is a human psychology. What we own that we possess. Whether corpus way or animus? It becomes very difficult to find out shortcomings in a thing which we own. We go blind to see any drawback since we are attached to it. Sometimes even if the mistakes are seen we ignore about our own weaknesses. And this is not going to be honest. Here we become dishonest.

Every person on this earth has a kind of self-motivation to reach the heights in his life. Heights in one's life could only be reached by honest means. There are heights of self-satisfaction, attainment and salvation. Why do we are supposed to be honest to our self and also to be just and fair while judging ourselves? We come across societal moral degradation all around. People are seen doing acts in their day to day lives which are degrading and corrupting human behavior. Human sufferings on this earth are manmade. We fail to judge the consequences of our wrongful acts and keep continuing to commit that. Failing to judge is not innocent but it is deliberate. We keep doing such acts with malicious intent since we deliberately wanted to do that knowing it fully well that such act is going to cause harm to others.

Why do we remain deliberately ignorant of our own weakness and faults? Overlooking our weaknesses is not going to help us out in any manner. You also forget that it is going to harm you only. May be you are ignorant of this harm too. This attitude is damaging. If you are vigilant then your mind keeps an honest watch over your activities whether rightful or wrongful. Mind naturally makes a judgment in a most impartial manner and passes it on to you to work upon it. You might have perceived it that your mind vigilantly signals good but since your thought process is badly influenced by your ulterior motives you act wrongfully in your words and deeds. The simplest way to identify weaknesses is that you should not behave with others the way you do not like others to behave with you. What is not good for you cannot be good for others? We start criticizing others when they do any wrongful act. But the similar wrongful act we start justifying when we are caught doing that. In fact this is not ignorance but is deliberately intentional act when you willfully fail to judge your actions. Make it a point that when you are not honest in judging yourself then you are not expected to be honest to others. That is where our individual and social perceptions go wrong.

That could be a pertinent question as to why do we need to be that sensitive in judging ourselves, whereas other people are least concerned about it? The answer is very simple. Kindly watch the social behavior very carefully in and around you. Feel no hesitation in admitting this bitter truth that there is a deep moral crisis present day society is suffering from. You should be honest enough in your observations for the kind of prevalent moral degradation in modern society of today which claims to be of high social and economic status. This is disappointing where children due to lack of proper institutional facilities are forced to starve right from their early childhood. This is disappointing in the sense where children in social system starve it could not be a strong system, would be hollow to its core. Dishonest and degrading thought process in the society not only makes an adverse impact to the persons individually but it has an adverse collective impact simultaneously. This is a matter of serious concern. How any nation is going to be strong one unless we all judiciously introspect? Introspection is nothing but an impartial witnessing of your wrongful deeds and resolving with determination to not to repeat again. Yes…!!! Off course, introspect good ones too for contributing to future generations. Have you ever analyzed your deeds? Or had there been any occasion for you to criticize yourself for the deeds you feel to be wrong ones? Self-criticism is not an easy task. There are people very rare who like to listen to their criticism. Introspection is a strong medium of self-criticism. You need to introspect daily on regular basis particularly at a time when your mind is completely transparent. The need would be that you identify your faults and mistakes. Keep overlooking your mistakes may cost you heavily when there would be no time left to rectify your mistakes. Even if you happen to repent, this is not going to help you. After introspection you came across the kind of pictures was quite disturbing. The option now left would be either you remain disturbed or you start connecting the pictures to better improve upon and proceed further.

Judging yourself honestly would be a state of your mind which is not only going to give you the strength but it would show you the ways also to rectify your mistakes and never to repeat. How would you feel when you are able to catch your mistakes? Definitely disturbed feel of mind or being ashamed of it even. How you need to counter your weaknesses? This decision is to be taken by you. Because despite you identify them, if you are not working upon them to bring into your personality then you fail in properly judging yourself. Rest assure of it. Furthermore, you have identified your weaknesses and you made sincere efforts to remove them, never feel confident that you have won. It would be a winning situation for you only when you are able to replace and substitute your weakness by a virtue inside you. Keep ensuring that your virtues are not again going to be overpowered by other weaknesses. By practicing it regularly you would find one day that the virtues have made permanent abode in your personality. It was possible because you judged yourself honestly. You might have seen many fighting with despair. They failed in sincerely making any effort to introspect themselves, identify their weakness and substitute them with virtues. Being innocent is not blameworthy but being deliberate is going to prove to be harmful to you.

"We start criticizing others when they do any wrongful act. But the similar wrongful act we start justifying when we are caught doing that. In fact this is not ignorance but is deliberately intentional act when you willfully fail to judge your actions. Make it a point when you are not honest in judging yourself then you are not expected to be honest to others."

————————————————

43

WHEN NOT TO SPEAK

Speaking is good. Keeping silence is equally good. When you speak you come out with words to communicate with. Sometimes words need to be acted upon. An officer commands his subordinates with the help of spoken words with an obvious motive that action should be initiated. Off course if action has not been initiated by subordinates as commanded then it would amount to an act of indiscipline. Does it mean, not speaking induces no action? Actions so induced may be positive or negative. Good actions are beneficial to the public at large. Bad actions are going to be harmful as well. Speaking well or speaking bad has its own sense. Or better not to speak when it is sensed to be inducing to a harmful action. But how long one needs to keep silent specifically when he witnesses that things are going beyond limits when he chooses not to speak? It happens on occasions when you are in the habits of avoiding to speak the other person goes on speaking using provocative words to you. You have the option to speak out or not to speak. You do not speak. The other person goes abusive crossing all the boundaries. Now that is the limit. People may ask, are you still left with options? No option, but to speak. Or still to keep silent. That is a challenging situation such person is going to encounter with. What others are expecting from you under such circumstances? You could have replied back in equally strong terms. You may justify your silence in a very philosophical sense. People may call your coward then. Better to keep quiet. You are not supposed to give explanation to everybody. People are no body to give you the kind of certificate they feel.

Let us always keep this very fact in mind that being argumentative all the time is not the way. You are not speaking may induce others feel like that either you are ignorant about it or you are not intelligent enough to understand the things so you are unable to properly speak out. What to say, people may go on discussing about your silence as amounting to some confession. You know you better than anybody else. It is your inner conscience which matters you much. Your own satisfaction brings you the complete peace of mind. You understand much better that wasting of your energy is of no use in satisfying the dirty minds. It is always better to remain silent rather winning out unnecessary arguments. The way money begets money in the similar manner words beget words. You want to speak out to be very precise. Those who wish to provoke you they would keep exchanging words unmindfully and without caring for the level of words they have used. If you also go on exchanging words, that is what they wanted. They are able to win their game and you go the looser. The energy of your mind and body is very precious. You have to care for it. Do not allow others to enter your mind and play with your precious energy. You need to save this energy within you and to speak out at an opportune time when your spoken words are needed most to deal with wrongful explanation of words and in protecting interests of a greater cause. Words only are not the limit, you know. On much bigger canvas of the world platform you have to imprint your words. So save them and do not engage yourself in unnecessary and unproductive talks. You have lot of many other challenges to handle with in your life.

Have you ever experienced the level of consciousness within you, when you are practicing silence? And compare the level of consciousness you feel when you are engaging yourself in unnecessary arguments on being provoked by others. When you speak out words but they are not properly communicative. Reasons could be of different levels of understanding. Sometimes words are communicated properly but understood differently. Words are also communicated defectively causing lot of damage to your reputation. Reason being that you did not speak consciously. You are a sensitive person so it affected you too. Why to speak out unconsciously and disturb yourself? Rather than choose when not to speak and feel content. Philosophical sense of silence has a different meaning. Silence induces you to go much deeper into your consciousness. The level of communication through silence is on a much higher level. It is possible for those only who are able to catch higher frequencies of your communication level. Be the best communicator of highest level. You should not forget that silence speaks louder than word. Off course, such loudness could be audible to those only who are up to that higher level. It would be of no use to others who are not able to catch the vibrations of what you speak. To be silent is miraculous in the sense that it is not easy for everybody to develop the skill as to when to speak and when to keep silent? You would realize this very fact that to keep speaking on unnecessary issues amounts not only wastage of energy but wastage of words too. Wasting of words may appear to be quite peculiar. But that's a true fact. Words are also wasted. When words are wasted they mean a lot for you. May be this has no meaning for the other person. Make it a point that words are your strength. You never mean to lose your strength in wasting your words by involving yourself in unnecessary arguments.

You have witnessed strength of words during political speeches. They are damaging also arousing to social unrest. Battles have been fought as a result of encounter with words between world leaders, thereby causing irreparable loss to innocent lives. Political leaders are very clever in the sense when to speak and what to speak? But they do not appear to be that clever when not to speak in larger public good. May be they are deliberate in this sense. No doubt, you may not be able to carry with your political career by keeping silent. You would have to speak out explaining your achievements to the people at the same time attacking the opposition. But this is no political discipline in its true letters and spirit. It is 'power politics' attempting to remain in power by any means instead of engaging in 'welfare politics'. Welfare is only possible when what you speak, you mean it. World leaders today are known for speaking something and doing just opposite to it. Their words loose strength since they fail to choose when not to speak. Words have enormous capacity provided they are arranged silently giving rise to creative work. All the great literary works and invention are created through silence only. Thinking and keep creating. Social reformers are best combinations of what they think they speak in larger social good. Advocates would fail if they do not speak their cases. You speak when you are so required to speak and choose when not to speak.

"Wasting of words may appear to be quite peculiar. But that's a true fact. Words are also wasted. When words are wasted they mean a lot for you. May be this has no meaning for the other person. Make it a point that words are your strength. You never mean to lose your strength in wasting your words by involving yourself in unnecessary arguments."

––––––––––––––––––––––––

44

MIND YOUR THOUGHTS

Thinking mind makes a distinction between animals and human beings. But it should never mean that animals do not think. There are very typical kinds of instances to show that animals do think and act so conspicuously even to beat around the human mind. Human thoughts are so systematic and in a well arranged manner which establishes ultimate superiority over animals. The moment it deviates the thought process is spoiled right from the beginning. The systematic pattern behind thinking process could be influence by moral standards of not only the family but also of the existing society in which the person lives. Social morality and economic morality are the most potent factors compelling thinking patterns of a man. A man suffering through acute poverty conditions would under no circumstances be in a position to come out with pleasant thoughts. He would come out with thoughts studded with all pain. Think of a society with its majority of people who are socio-economically weak. How could we think of such societies with thoughts full of vigor? Negative thoughts are bound to crop up in the mind of a society which is starving. Please do not expect from them that they are able to control themselves to take all precautions while speaking out their thoughts. Starving stomachs give rise to empty minds. Instead of creative thinking such minds could be violent. No blame should be fixed upon them for their violent thoughts.

Thoughts could be positive as well as negative depending upon the circumstances prevailing around. Thoughts generate force. It would be creative force if thought positively. All of a sudden it would turn to be damaging force the moment thoughts go negative. Have you ever experienced potency of your thoughts? Potency is in the sense that flow of thoughts in your mind is capable enough in helping you to achieve your goals. Your potent thoughts generate the needed will power to succeed. If you happen to read life history of world leaders you would find that they could succeed because they were driven by the force of their thoughts. They could achieve what they wanted to achieve. Positive thoughts infuse inspiration by resorting to those skills which would be necessary to get that goal. Positivity of thoughts is well deserved to remain positive not only for you but to be positive for others too. Imagine a situation where people think negative about you and keep looking for any such opportunity to damage you. Yes...!!! They damage you also. No doubt it's quite human that you also start thinking to counter them with negative thoughts to seek revenge. To get moved with such thoughts is very easy but to get rid of them is much difficult, making you pass through restless days and nights. Once you are in grip with negative thoughts it is testing times for you to get out of such thoughts.

Getting successful in your life and getting successful in your career are two different things. You may be highly successful in your career but at the same time you could be a failure in your life. The most pertinent question here is that whatever your career may be either good or bad, but you have to be successful in your life. Success of your life lies in the fact that you attained a state of mind where you remain positive even with those people who were negative against you and at times they were active in causing loss to you. You mustered the courage to bear the loss. That is a well thought strength on your part. You would feel further strengthened in being not negative towards them by saving much of your energy being wasted as negative energy. Seeking revenge from them is not the ultimate goal of your life. Leave such negative people the way they are. Feel pity about them. You will be a big failure in your life once you decide to be after them. Instead you are concentrating and focusing your mind strictly around your positive thoughts you will feel the influx of mental strength and the vigor in making you successful they way you wanted to achieve the goals of your life.

Apply your thoughts basically when you feel weak and go out of vigor following influx of negative thoughts in your mind. Yes...!!! This is true. May be deliberately you are not watchful of these changes in your body and mind but when observed minutely you well find that you are not feeling good within you. You find that you have been overpowered by sadness and depressive thoughts immediately after you allowed negative thoughts entering to your mind. Your body language reflects anger also full with despair. Do you think that these things are good for your body and mind? No...!!! Never. Once you are overpowered by these negative impulses it would be getting very difficult for you to get yourself out of it. When you possess negative thoughts for others to harm them, whether or not you are in position to harm them, but definitely you are going to harm yourselves. Further chances would be that you may never be able to reach to your goal. No doubt, I am in complete agreement with you that how this could be possible to keep oneself content with positive thoughts against all odds, especially to face such dirty people who are out with their negative acts to harm you? Very difficult task and challenging too, in testing you to maintain a balance so that negative thoughts are not getting any chance to dominate your positive mind set. That would be great for you when you are equipped with this strength.

Mind your thoughts, I mean that you should be watchful about your thoughts, as you pass with your days. People may attempt to bring negative thoughts to you that are their habit. You should be with your open mind to retain positive thoughts with you each day and leaving behind the negative thoughts. You need to practice each day and train your mind to forget the negativity of people said to you or done to you. No doubt, this practice is very difficult but it is possible. Starting your days with your family members with positive set of mind, meeting people at the workplace with a focused positivity and a never mind attitude to the negative talks of your colleagues. You have set certain goals in your life. Majority of people around you keep making efforts to restrain you from becoming successful. This is common tendency among people when they see that you are doing well, what they cannot do, they would play damaging to spoil your efforts. This is going to be the real challenge that despite all you are maintaining balancing of your thoughts in such a manner that without bothering for their all negativity you kept moving ahead with more tough and strong. You emerged as victorious in real sense. Now you feel confident physically and mentally, with abundant peace of mind and without any stress. That is how such people are defeated and left behind to their mercy. You will also experience that your mind reaches the stage where it is not burdened with feeling of anger and vengeance enabling you to achieve your life goals.

"No doubt I am in complete agreement with you that how this could be possible to keep oneself content with positive thoughts against all odds, especially to face such dirty people who are out with their negative thoughts to harm you. Very difficult and challenging too."

45

PURITY OF YOUR CHILDHOOD

Our children are the most pure form of our humanity. They are pure by the simple logic that their mind thinks and acts without any prejudice against anybody. Why there is no prejudice in childhood? Why children are so pure? They know what they know. They speak what they have to speak. They do not know what is dishonesty? They do not know how to be dishonest? That is why they do not have any miseries, always happy full with cheers. Then who puts dishonesty into their mind? How do they learn to suppress their pure thoughts and replace them by dirty ones? The society and surrounding environment play a decisive role in polluting the purity of childhood. Right from their childhood the children are made to learn that honesty is the best policy. But such learning later prove to be of no use when the same system goes to be dishonest.

A child grows young by very minutely observing all that. He gets no plausible answers to his queries arising out in his mind as to why society goes that dishonest? The same set of minds which taught the child to be honest, on occasions makes them to learn how to be dishonest? The child looks that dishonesty yields results very fast and in a much easier manner. He also observes at the same time that those who are honest are put to many hardships by those who are dishonest. People who are honest are denied from what they deserve to be? Such a scenario makes an adverse impact on growing mind of the child. More worse is that our social system also does not possess any such mechanism preventing such thinking pattern of the child. It becomes very difficult some times to understand if childhood lessons of honesty being the best policy had been in fact pure, then how come such people who are following this policy intact and are honest, put to such hardships? This discourages the mind of a growing child. He is not ready, as noticed on a very large scale, to be put to hardships for the sake of being honest.

Every civilization writes its own governing principles. To become strong nations draw their own constitutions. The condition would be that they have to behave according to the constitutional parameters they have drawn for themselves. The moment such nations or societies go against their governing principles, the nation or society goes weak and weak. Merely preaching of governing principles would be of no use unless they are put into practice in their true letters and spirit. We preach our children to behave in a principled manner but when it comes to practice for ourselves we fail to do that. We forget then the famous lines of William Wordsworth that the child is the father of the man. We are directly responsible to spoil the purity of their childhood by more preaching and less practicing to it. Childhood mind learns much faster than an adult mind. In similar way it is also spoiled much faster. Looking into the life of a person individually managing principles is very significant. By infusing such principles in them right from their childhood the society would be able to make children an ideal individual. The society would get expected results subject to the conditions that it also continues to be ideal and behaves following managing principles. Present society is suffering from complete lack of mutual trust among its members. This did not happen overnight. The situations became worse with the passage of time when society apparently went careless in protecting their childhood. When the child goes young he imitates the adult society. If he finds that society does not have any principles he is bound to deviate from his rightful path, making his life much chaotic.

Where purity of the childhood has been built in and we are able to carry it through our adulthood, our life has to be pleasant, full of honestly and beauty. The purity completely sets in our life actions. We may come up with certain conflicting situations in our life. We may not find immediate solutions when we look to the governing principles. We then go by the dictates of our inner conscience. We find that our decision was absolutely correct under the given circumstances. Make it a point that your conscience always shows the right path provided you are ready to receive these impulses with a pure heart. Your conscience continuously signals the right way but you deliberately ignore. You can then well understand fate of your actions. Consider that you have received impulses of your inner conscience correctly but you look for more convenient means to act upon rather than by the means which could be though bit difficult but is going to yield better results. That is the problem, we prefer convenience than difficulties. Honestly speaking adversities make us stronger from within.

Being honest is total purity. It does not go by person's conveniences but it could be full with adversities too. We would be able to enjoy its purity only when we make ourselves ready to face the adversities if any. To begin with entire society, honesty is not individualistic. Where majority of people are honest in a society one can easily imagine the flow of purity of thoughts and well being of such society. Think of a society with absence of purity and practicing dishonesty. Think of children who are growing up in such a society. A society with moral order is possible only by a collective attitude. We find that collective attitude missing in society that is why the social disorder we are coming across. This sense of purity flows right from the childhood to the adulthood only when it is carried forward very carefully.

What I mean to submit before you is that maintaining of purity of the childhood is possible provided we are vigilant at different stages of our life strictly not allowing entry of any impurities within ourselves. We are pure when we are honest. We are pure when we are free from any greed, lust or anger. But is it that easy? All these factors of impurity directly affect the intellect of a person thereby he loses his capacity to think honestly. Thus he becomes dishonest. Watch it carefully you would find that childhood is free from all such impurities. That is why a child acts with purity of thoughts and intention. Adulthood would also be able to maintain the same purity if he is able to establish complete control over his greed, lust and anger. This is possible only by means of self-control mechanism and by rigorous practice. Protect the purity of your childhood. Positive learning of the childhood is very valuable asset not only for an individual but for the society as a whole spreading the fragrance of purity, joy, happiness all around.

"Think of a society with absence of purity and practicing dishonesty. Think of children who are growing up in such a society. A society with moral order is possible only by a collective attitude. We find that collective attitude missing in society that is why the social disorder we are coming across. The sense of purity flows right from the childhood to the adulthood only when it is carried forward very carefully."

46

FLYING WITH THOUGHTS

Where there is flow of thoughts in your mind you feel that there is life. A person's thought may be good or bad, they influence his personality. Where there is positive influence of thoughts it would be considered to be developmental face of his personality. Otherwise, negativity of personality sooner or later happens to be damaging. Do not we so realize that we live our life the way our mind wants? Meaning thereby that either we are able to live our life or else we live our mind. Living our mind means our life is similar to the thoughts at that time in our mind. Our thoughts are reflected in our daily behavior. Good thoughts in the mind make our life good. It would be just reverse if bad thoughts are there in the mind. When people are preoccupied with thoughts, whether good or bad, they are not able to live in their present. Thoughts are either bundle of post memories or visualization for future life. Past memories pull you backwards in time which is already passed away. They do not take you to the present moments in which you are living. Your future visualizations give you thoughts for future which is yet to materialize in your life. Means your thoughts make you live either in past which is already dead or in future which is still a dream. But you have no option but to move with it. You feel for a moment, you will find that your mind is just a flow of thoughts. Flying with thoughts is a human imagination and this paves the way for creations in future.

The past which we feel is gone is not gone in fact. Past is the root which makes the base for our future establishments. The condition would be that by living in present we need to maintain strong link between the past and the future. Off course then, we would be able to enjoy our present.

Flying with thoughts is quite natural for us. It should not be understood in the sense that thoughts for future achievements are dreams only. Dreams for individual advancement are the images which an individual intends to achieve in his future life. What he would intend to achieve in future he would start making his sincere efforts from today itself i.e. his present. Dreams are not only dreams. Your mind is not flying through any state of unconsciousness. Your mind is full of awareness provided that it is sensitive towards its future achievements. Take for example you desire to be a great man. You also understand that being great is a tough task. It is a continuous thought process for a man for years altogether when he starts orienting his mind in such a manner so that he gets his target done. An author keeps flying with his thoughts, something about his memories of the past or dreams of his future perceptions and translates into his wittings in larger interest of human welfare. His thoughts for establishing brotherhood in the society among the individuals with different faiths, for establishing peace on this earth are not just momentary thoughts but are result of conscious thought process in the present and of the past.

Your past has just gone but that is not wasted. It is not wasted in the sense that you remain aware of your past mistakes. You were conscious that such mistakes are not repeated in future. That is enough. It would not mean that you were living in past. If you are not looking back to your past how could you be in a position to catch your mistakes? Then you would not be in a position to rectify your mistakes even. How about achievements? How about betterments then? History reveals that for a man approaching to be great mistakes are bound to happen. The person did commit mistakes or mistakes just happened to him, both are the two different things. If he did commit mistakes, he did it knowingly. There would be lesser tendency for rectification. He would do it again. Where mistakes have just occurred to him, which he never intended, there would be every possibility for improvement in future. Then such man would proceed on his way to become great. This he would be able to do with the help of his past mistakes and thoughts of the past which kept storming into his mind day and night.

If thought is for human then yes, we live our mind in the sense that we need to take a decision to not to keep sitting and looking for the thoughts. Once you have thoughts in your mind you have to identify yourself with those thoughts and start working on them to ensure getting desired results and again ready with identifying your thoughts. In this case your internal bodily mechanism gets accelerated. It is motivated by your belief inside you that, yes, you can do it. You believe that you can achieve targets of your life. You believe that you can do something for the people who are denied by the system. You believe to work for establishing brotherhood\and peace on this earth. You desire to become great that people remember you after you die. It is in fact flow of your beliefs which are rooted in your thoughts. Having desires in one's life is not wrong. The desired could be for personal gain or for common good. If you desire to become a scientist for welfare of the mankind it should be welcomed. If you desire to be leader for common man for protection of his interests that is very nice. That is the need of the hour. You come forward with your welfare thoughts and planning, this world awaits you with full honors. You take such calculated steps towards achieving your targets when your thoughts and mind convinces you that you have to take lead without making much delay. Your thoughts are also influenced by prevailing situations across the globe, whether social, economic or political. You are not able to keep yourself aloof without responding to all that happening around. You might have experienced that your logical mind bursts out and cries for solutions. You could not stop yourself from reacting out when you kept watching that all is not going well in the society. Well, you had the option before you to remain silent with thinking, let that happen what is happening. Why should I be bothered about it? It is not going to harm me anyway. It is none of my business then to think about it or apply my mind even. But believe it that is not possible for a person like you. You are not self-centered looking only for your vested interests. You are a man who is worried about public good. Your flow of thoughts would be in larger public interest. Present global scenario is in desperate need for a leadership which is more thinkers and people's welfare oriented rather than a leader who is more political. Your flow of thoughts would take you to the path of greatness. But you do not want to be great in the sense that you want to dedicate yourself for the work you have chosen to perform. You are flying with your thoughts.

"Your thoughts are also influenced by prevailing situations across the globe, whether social, economic or political. You are not able to keep yourself aloof without responding to all that happening around. You might have experienced that your logical mind bursts out and cries for solutions. You could not stop yourself from reacting out when you kept watching that all is not going well in the society."

47

LIVING FOR OTHERS

There are sayings that if a man is living for himself only, what is then difference between a man and an animal? An animal also lives for itself. But to my understanding this saying is not fair in the sense that you would find animals which are more faithful to their masters in comparison to men. In a society like today where we come across heavy moral degradation it becomes very difficult to even rely upon the others. Albert Einstein, the great scientist always believed in a life which is worth living and has been lived for others. We in a society are completely self-centered. We only concern with our own vested interests and do things for our own personal gains. The moment we are able to protect our interests we stop thinking further. Do we get time to think for others or to live for others? Why a man has become so self-centered? This is big question which needs to be answered. I do not know whether such questions troubles one? If it so happens then how does he respond to it? Do we consider that a scientist lives for others? Whether an author lives for others? It may be your perception as to how many of us are able to benefit ourselves from advancement of science or from any work of literature? I think the conclusion would be quite painful.

Do we really wish to live for others? We need to make category of people we wish to live for. Have you witnessed the glaring inequalities in your society? The kind of social and economic inequality. A society which believes in caste discrimination and discrimination based upon religious faiths. Such social divisions are not going to establish any congenial atmosphere on this earth. How the achievements of a scientist are going to help out a man who is suffering from starvation? That's right scientific inventions must go on. That too is for betterment of the mankind. But there are majority of people on this earth who are still looking for fulfillment of their day to day basic minimum necessities. How any literary work is going to help them with their stomachs empty? Poverty generates crimes. Poverty generates revolutions. A child is born in a poor family. Please do not blame him for his poverty conditions. Please do not blame a man for his caste because he is born in a low caste. He never knew about his caste when he was child. People made him know that he was low a caste when he grew young. Now he is realizing this fact that people are keeping at distance from him for his low caste. The caste ridden society does not support him. He was born poor, he continues to be poor and he will die poor, he knows it. No one from within society came forward to support him. He understood that. No one helps, one has to fight his own destiny, and this became his conviction when he was mature.

Sufferings have their own impact over persons. The sufferings which are by virtue of nature one has no control over it but manmade sufferings are culpable. This is due to societal discrimination among individuals. Our society would be heading for an eventual collapse if prevailing situations are allowed to continue like this. Children would ask that they were hungry, they cried but this society gave them nothing to eat. They were thirsty, they cried but this society did not allow them to take water. They were shivering in biting cold but the society never bothered for it. They were sick but we did not care to look after them. Who would come forward to give reply to these questions? Where are the caretakers of this social system? Did we live for ourselves only? Did we live for them even once? No. . . . Not. We have no easy answers for these questions. We should never forget this fact that we are also sailing in the same boat and would reach to the same destination. The only difference would be that may be something more or something less. It may be something good or something bad. One day all would meet to the same fate. Poverty means scarcity even to the extent of earning one's livelihood. May be on occasions nothing to eat or drink for the sake of survival. People with abundance of money go wasting it like anything for the sake of their luxury and comforts. There should be no objection to anybody for a man living luxurious life out of his hard earned money. But the same authority cannot be conferred to individuals who have abundance of money for their luxuries earned by all corrupt means. This fact remains in constructive notice of the caretakers of the system but they also have their hands in gloves with. The majority sufferers who are already weak have no other option but to keep suffering and suffering and die a death which is not human like. This is a big curse on humanity. But who cares to live for others? No way.

Human sensitivity agitates the human mind. Their sufferings make such human to be sensitive for those people who are similarly subjected to such discriminatory, humiliations, poverty conditions and injustices of all kinds. It creates a feeling of compassion in them because they are able to feel their pains and adversities in life. They are moved within their heart to come forward to help them, to live for them as their resources so permit. It is not unusual that the governments fail to deliver human welfare measures for they are corrupt neck deep. Cases of large scale misappropriations in poverty alleviation schemes are well known. But after all they are our elected government, who stops us to pull them out if they fail to deliver public good? Why do we tolerate such corrupt governments which fail to live for their people? But we tolerate and wait that is the truth. At the same times we as a fellow citizen cannot escape from our responsibility. Off course, it is ethical to live for them and help them out. We do not do so. Whenever your mind feels agitating for others and the moment you start feeling another's pain, it makes you move to help them out. Feeling of love and compassion has been generated out of natural bonds of human impulses. If a man could be compassionate for animals then why not for fellow human beings? It would be my humble submission before you my friends that this earth one day would be worth living provided we start feeling that compassion to live for others.

"A child is born in a poor family. Please do not blame him for his poverty conditions. Please do not blame a man for his caste because he is born in a low caste. He never knew his caste when he was a child. People made him know that he was a low caste when he grew young. Now he is realizing this fact that people are keeping at distance from him for his low caste."

48

REACH LIFE DESTINATIONS

You live your life you reach to your destination. What is your destination? Who decides your destination? You see that you did all that to the best of your capacity and satisfaction to reach to your destination but could not. You wanted to be a doctor and serve the people by medical profession. Despite your sincere efforts you failed to reach to your destination to be a doctor. You were disappointed but you never lost your courage. You switched over your destination and started preparing to join civil services. You made your attempts by putting in hard labor but you failed. You were full of disappointment again. Nobody did answer to your queries in your mind. As to who decides your destination? You are putting in hard labor, what else? Now you feel yourself to be at cross roads to decide for yet another target of your life to be your next destination. You mustered your all courage to strike hard for your new venture. You were already suspicious as to what is going to happen next? Your past experiences were revealing the truth that whether you should be content only to perform the journey in a best possible manner? Or you should be equally worried for your destination too? You wanted to be a doctor, you failed. You wanted to be an administrator, you could not. You were confident by your heart that you made honest efforts but you did not get any answer as to why you failed to reach to your destination?

Now you are a practicing lawyer thinking for the reasons that you were left with no option but to join this profession for earning livelihood for your kids. You were doing good and working hard. You were good with your arguments during conduct of court proceedings. You had an untiring urge to keep earning knowledge so that you won cases for your clients. You earned your name in the profession to your satisfaction. Your advocacy profession by nature had a long gestation period to settle down and you were content with it to carry it on. To your utter surprise you came to learn one fine morning that being in profession of law was not going to be your final destination. You received an offer to join teaching profession, to be an academician to profess the jurisprudence to law students. You were put again at the crossroads in your life. What to do now? You were satisfied with your profession in law. How come this offer to deal with? You got stuck with great dilemma of your life. You had a strong inclination in favor of practicing law. You knew that once accepting the offer to join academics, you would not be able to appear for your clients before the courts. Whether practicing in law was your destination? Or else teaching in law was going to be your destination once for all. You could never sense that when your mind consented for academics, whereas you had your first love for practicing the law. You surrendered which you could never know. You tried what the best you could give to your student. It was the jurisprudence which was nicely mixed with finer points of theory of law and its practical dimensions. You made your students to nicely understand that there was a lot of difference between the theory and practice of law.

Your jurisprudential teachings made you to go in deep about the tenets of justice whether it was social, economic or political. You then witnessed people suffering from glaring social injustice. Frightening economic disparity was prevailing all around. A big number of people were forced to live below the poverty line. You were convinced that for all that injustice the politically elected governments, their defective policy making and its careless implementation were responsible. It all went deep to pain you heart. Majority of people were denied from their legal rights. They were subjected to acute discrimination of all kinds. Justice administration and justice delivery system was of no meaning.

It was just ornamental and accessible to those who were resourceful and could afford that. Looking to all this, while responsible ones remained busy in playing dirty politics for power, your heart cried and cried deep. You decided that you cannot remain a silent spectator and that it was not your destination. You then entered into active national politics who knows that it was your final destination indeed? You were again encountering with a big unanswered question as what your destination was? Whether your desire for destination was fulfilled the way you wanted? Or whatever the varied kind of journey you performed in your life was responsible for determining your further destinations? Now you were in a position to realize that you were mature enough to understand that it was the journey in fact and not the destination which played crucial role in keep you changing. Your journey is more significant than your desire for destination. Keep making your life journey with honesty you are bound to reach the destinations of greatness. The world needs you in this hour of turmoil. Come on…!!! Now your destination was to work for welfare of the poor unprivileged weaker sections of the mankind and you were happy with it.

Therefore simple answer to the queries would be that depending upon life situations your conscious mind decides your destination. Under changing circumstances and need of the hour your sensitive mind equips you to target the next destination and reach up to it. Your destination keeps changing according to sweet or bitter experiences of your journey. Performing the journey to your destination is also much dependent upon your state of mind. It is your mindset that you derive much happiness by the struggle you made rather than the goal you reached. This kind of feeling would never make you worry even if you could not achieve your goal for various reasons. Enjoy your journey by putting your best, your actions must be packed with quality never be worried about what your destination is going to be. Failure could be a bitter truth of life. Your journey could be full of competitions. At times you could also be among the losers. Failures are necessary ingredients for determined destinations. Never bother about your adversaries. Perform your journey without looking back. Your destination would be worth you felt proud of it. Your life is a journey and your best destinations are human welfare, happiness and peace for the mankind on this earth.

"Your journey is more significant than your desire for destination. Keep making your life journey with honesty you are bound to reach the destinations of greatness. The world needs you in this hour of turmoil. Come on...!!! Now your destination was to work for welfare of the poor unprivileged weaker sections of the mankind and you were happy with it."

49

YOUR GRACEFUL MIND

We need to make our mind graceful since it is the centre where there is continuous flow of different kinds of thoughts. The thoughts could be of the nature which are harmful to others as well as to one's own self. Like a man has certain desires without understanding the fact those desires are beyond his reach. He still keeps making such desires and remains full of worries. A man has certain intention to do something. What a person intends to first he thinks about it and forms an idea which he implements subsequently. When a person does something intentionally, he gives other person a reason to believe that he is doing such act with full knowledge. So later he has no opportunity to rebut that he did it innocently. Presence of intention shows that the person did it knowingly. What do you imagine, is not you, but your thoughtful mind? Your imaginations would come out to be true provided they are on sound base and pursued honestly and thoughtfully.

Why we need our mind to be graceful? It is the compulsive force of mind which makes your body to move. Consider your body to be a vehicle. Your body as a vehicle would not move unless your mind is so prepared for it. Mind contains needed instruments out of the experiences it possesses from time to time and then it so decides as to what could be the rightful action making it therefore to be graceful. Our life is full of negative actions as well as positive actions. The grace lies in the fact that your actions do not put you in any awkward position in your life. When a man is sleeping, his mind is in a dormant stage therefore his body is unaware of any conscious action. A man laying in his bed in a coma condition for months or even years altogether his mind as an instrument has completely lost its control over the body. Due to this malfunctioning of mind, coma stage persists and the man is not in a position to act upon through his body. In a person lying in coma, his mind goes nonfunctional and you would notice that his physical grace is lost. Without human existence the body has no movement though the person is living and not declared dead. Thus the crux of the entire note is that our mind is though most sophisticated but a very delicate instrument, so always needed to be handled with utmost care and precaution. With a view to enjoy full grace of mind in one's life it is felt necessary to understand the functioning of mind. Researches have revealed that the human mind is always in search of positivity like happiness, joy, peace and the like. That is the grace of mind which great people of our times have enjoyed. It is the human lust and greed which spoils the mind towards negativity and the gracefulness of the mind is lost.

Have you ever experienced carefully on occasions, when your life is not able to enjoy happiness then can you feel happy? Have you ever felt as to what is the nature of happiness? Does the happiness lie in the objects of the world? Whether this world is beautiful or the beauty lies in the eyes of beholder? Really it is a very difficult question to reply. It is the eye only which perceives beauty and sends signals to mind. The objects do not give happiness where the mind is incapable to experience the same. It is the mind which is the seat of happiness in true sense. Many a times you might have seen that you are sitting with a disturb mind. There are objects of happiness kept just in front of you but your mind keeps irritating. You are not happy till your mind gets out of the disturbance and becomes normal. May be the object remains full with joy and happiness but your mind seems to have attained the level of satisfaction and it goes calm, experiencing happiness from within. But it is a temporary phase and the mind again starts searching for the objects to be happy. This could be seen as if the mind has gone dependent on the objects and in the absence of those objects the minds developed a tendency to be sad. This is not welcome.

The gracefulness of the mind lies deep within, in the fact that our mind has the rare capacity to develop its own internal mechanism to remain happy and joyful. It does not depend upon any object searching for the joy. But the requirement is that we have to support the mind by regular practice in its effort to be full with joy even in the absence of objects. That is possible but by passing through rigorous practice. People get attached with objects like food. Try to feel the level of happiness for a man who is hungry, when he gets food to get to his empty stomach. Taste of food has no meaning for him. He enjoyed like none other man, who is looking for a tasty food and remains unsatisfied and sad. The mind enjoyed the food gracefully even if the food was not tasty since the man needed the food badly. Here in this case it was the perception of internal mechanism of the mind which did not depend upon tasty food and was comparatively much happier. That's the graceful mind.

Conclusion goes that make your mind free from any such dependence which could make it sorrow. That is true, whether tasty food or simple food, object has to be there. Now keeping in mind the need of the hour the mind gracefully chooses one, which is a greater source of happiness. This would only be possible when you are leaving your mind independent of any urge and giving it full freedom of choice in given situations. Once the freedom given, the grace of mind enables itself to search out the true source of joy and happiness. This becomes possible due to pure state of mind. We should not forget that mind has its own likes and dislikes, accordingly it pursues the objects. Even though the object may appear to be good but the mind could have its own reasons for its dislike. We need to feel and respect the approach of mind. Only in consonance with our perceptive mind, we would be able to enjoy the happiness. If we make ourselves to be attached with the object despite dislikes from the mind we are making the mind disgraceful.

"People get attached with objects like food. Try to feel the level of happiness for a man who is hungry, when he gets food to get to his empty stomach. Taste of food has no meaning for him. He enjoyed

like none other man, who is looking for a tasty food and remains unsatisfied and sad. The mind enjoyed the food gracefully even if the food was not tasty since the man needed the food badly. Here in this case it was the perception of internal mechanism of the mind which did not depend upon tasty food and was comparatively much happier. That's the graceful mind."

———————————————

50

NOT FOR IGNORANCE

Gaining knowledge but not practicing the knowledge in our behavior are two different things. One could be a knowledgeable person in the sense that he could clear a written examination of national importance while others could not. Yes…!!! He has the required knowledge that is why he could succeed and was much ahead of others in the competition. It was his knowledge of the subject concerned which enabled him to pass the examination and make him enjoy the pleasure of success. Now the pertinent question is whether same is good for life's examinations as well? Life is a big journey full with examinations on every step. If one is negligent about his steps there is every possibility that he may fail to live his life successfully. Is it possible that one who is considered to be a man with good knowledge but he suffers from ignorance of different nature? Why not…!!! Yes…!!! It is possible. There are people considered to be full with knowledge suffering from various sick mentalities. Our literature keep emphasizing that honesty is the best policy. But who cares? Honesty has nothing to do with person's knowledge. He could be the most dishonest and corrupt man. He would be seen preaching honesty and practicing of morality by others but just contrary to that he has been found crossing all the limits of immorality. Do we say him that he is ignorant or he is deliberate? His greedy character makes him not only ignorant about his good knowledge but deliberate too.

Bookish knowledge cannot be equated with worldly knowledge. Kindly compare between the knowledge which has been acquired and the knowledge which has been gained through experience. It is not a technical knowledge but one acquires it through day to day worldly experience. This is also called as personal insight of a man. One can hear persons telling about receiving some information by way of intuition. It is my personal experience that intuitions are correct. It is scientifically linked with vibrations of your thinking process and passes through wave mechanism. In technologically advanced communication system of today you might have experienced personally on number of occasions that the moment you remember any of your relative or friend at the same time you receive a phone call from his side. You were surprised over the chain of events as to how come it all happened? You just remembered him and there was a phone call. You tell him also that you were just remembering him, by the time he makes you a call to your utter surprise. It is just not any matter of coincidence. You have a kind of intuition of happening of certain incident well in advance. You see by the time that incident takes place. You become surprised as to how come it all happened? How could you know the happening of things well in advance? How could this came to your mind? The person you just remembered and you received his phone call. Whether your friend got some intuition that you are remembering him? He made a phone call to you. If you happen to think minutely you would find that this is the knowledge you acquired by the heights of intellectuality. This has ultimately been converted into spiritualistic height. At the highest levels of spiritual character one becomes in a position to acquire intuitive knowledge. Have you observed birds and animals behaving uniquely and making peculiar type of noises which are indicative of some natural calamity? They have intuitive capacity to gain the knowledge in advance that some disturbing crisis relating to nature is going to happen. Science also admits this fact. Kindly notice, despite the fact that these birds and animals do not possess knowledge like we human beings but they are not at all ignorant. By means of intuitive sense they get the knowledge that the nature is going to be in trouble so they remain alert.

Our atmosphere is full with moving waves of different frequency. The waves we release in the form of voices, movements, the forms of communication etc. Human mind also has this capacity to catch these waves and communications subject to the condition that we practice to the extent to develop that capacity up to the level of frequency and its wavelength. The capacity has been achieved is indicated by the spiritual experiences you start perceiving. You receive impulses in the form of intuitions. The conclusion is that no ignorance stage follows after the knowledge stage. Therefore, you have to keep gaining knowledge of different kinds because you are not for ignorance. Ignorance of anything is no excuse for a human mind. Once you are up with knowledge honestly there is no reason for you to be ignorant. That's what in simple words we refer to that ignorance nothing is but lack of knowledge. Lacking big in knowledge means bigger is going to be the ignorance.

You are a human being you want to be happy and peaceful in your life. Precondition for that would be your spiritual attainment. Your spiritual quest would be indicative of the fact that you are in search of happiness and peace of mind. The four strong pillars of spiritual attainment would be truth, perseverance, wisdom and chastity. If any of these pillars is not balancing properly than the platform of spiritual attainment over these pillar is going to be shaky and weak. In that event you are going to be ignorant in your worldly knowledge. You would be weak despite the fact that you are strong subjectively up with knowledge. Truth is the kind of basic knowledge for human beings. There is no need to say that the truth has strength. Practice the truth and experience the kind of strength within you. Observe such people who avoid truth and watch their facial psychology and their body language. They would always be looking like scared of something unseen of. Feel the purity of body and your mind by practicing the truth. Truth is tough but possible. It is perseverance in the sense that you have to practice the truth not for a day or two but throughout your life. This is combined strength of truth and perseverance that today you find yourself in a position to talk to any person with an eye to eye contact. This brings within you the needed wisdom to pierce through as to what is right and what is wrong. It strengthens your urge for justness and fairness, to let the truth prevail and nothing but the truth. Now you see knowledge begets knowledge in turn begets no ignorance. The last pillar chastity automatically gets its way inside you. You can say this is the net result of other three knowledge pillars. The chastity of birds and animals has developed in them no ignorant intuitive sense. You also can. You are for knowledge not for ignorance.

"Have you observed birds and animals behaving uniquely and making peculiar type of noises which are indicative of some natural calamity? They have intuitive capacity to gain the knowledge in advance that some disturbing crisis relating to nature is going to happen. Science also admits this fact. Kindly notice, despite the fact that these birds and animals do not possess knowledge like we human beings but they are not at all ignorant. By means of intuitive sense they get the knowledge that the nature is going to be in trouble so they remain alert."

———————————————

51

PRACTICING IN YOU

There is a famous saying that practicing brings perfection in you. Thus practicing in you becomes very significant to gain perfection whether to your body or mind. You would have witnessed training sessions for sports persons. It is not that they organize training camps for practice during playing seasons only but with a view to keep them physically and mentally fit they keep regularly practicing during off season even. Sports are not completely physical but they do require a good calculative mind too while planning the game at the time of actual performance in fields. In today's era of professionalism the sports too have become much strategic. Looking to the opposite side and their game plan the other side too prepares its strategy well in advance to counter attack the opponent. By practicing the same shot over and again the players try to develop a kind of their muscle readiness which they term as 'muscle memory'. When they are in field actually and face varying situations of the game put forth by the opposition, there is no much time to for them to think over the opposition move then their 'muscle memory' comes to their rescue. They respond to opposition move quickly what they learnt during their practice session and win over the situation for sure. The lesson is that had they not been put themselves to regular practice they could not have developed the 'muscle memory' and would have failed to tackle the opposition move.

The 'muscle memory' has a direct relationship with 'brain memory' of an individual player. It is in fact the mind which has to respond quickly on the basis of those signals which have been stored in the 'muscle memory' of the player. The players who stay in competition practice their all possible similar shots for thousands of times without fail. They keep toning up their body and mind so tough that they are ever ready finding themselves fit to join with a winning attitude. A similar kind of practicing is needed for us as well in our body and mind. One may argue that it's an exclusively physical activity in case of sports persons therefore they may need a completely different kind of regular physical practice in comparison to those who perform more mental activity rather than physical. That is no doubt, true. But we tend to forget one very important thing that in a healthy body only dwells a healthy mind. Do not we feel that our aging mind needs a regular practice to remain young, imaginative and fertile? Yes…!!! We feel. Then how come it is going to be possible expecting a brain to be sharp enough without practicing much on it? If we want a working and sharp mind, it is not possible unless we keep sharpening it with regular and rigorous practice on it. Otherwise, sooner it would turn to be blunt. Our brain memory diminishes with the passage of time and off course, the age. We start developing a tendency to forget things. That's quite natural, what we term as aging factor. But by means of practicing on it regularly the impact of aging factor on our mind could be reduced to a considerable extent. It is my humble submission that this could be any body's experience for all the time. This could better be understood in terms of developing 'brain memory' in strict spiritual sense. So that the practicing mind keeps getting support from your body, thus a balancing mechanism between the body and the mind is strongly established.

For practicing of the mind, in our literatures there are tools provided. But the condition is that we should be open to adopt them in our life. For better results one would only be in a position to know once he decides to start practicing these tools and has the required patience to wait for the desired results. It would take time. Miracles are not going to happen. The practicing tools could be put in following order. Firstly, 'listening' to the teaching or reading them. There are sufficient quantities of literature available in the form of teachings from great thinkers. But we find that we do not possess much patience to listen to or develop reading habits. The result, we find that a big share of our population is not mentally that alert what they could have been expected to be. They do have the mental capacity but for lack of patience and interest in such teachings. Second tool is in the nature of 'contemplation'. Merely teachings are not enough and would not serve any purpose unless we contemplate on to such teachings once, twice, thrice or even more till we find our mind in a position to better analyze and understand those teachings in their proper sense. On true contemplation of such teachings you will feel from inside you a kind of restlessness to keep studying and practicing the teachings till it reaches through your skin to the bone marrow deep. It does not merely remain a teaching now you start debating on it not only within your own self but you do so outwardly too with other intellectuals.

You might have observed on number of occasions when you find yourself talking with you only on an amazing intellectual level. Debating any subject within ourselves is contemplation stage of human mind which takes him up to certain levels of derivations and conclusions. Finally, comes the tool of 'meditation' in which you have to work upon those derivations and the conclusions. To reach up to the level of meditating upon the outcome of those teachings which are found out of thorough contemplation, is the real pleasure in one's life. If one could achieve it by practicing, that is possible. It could be a life span time to keep practicing on with your body and mind and keep enjoying the fruits so acquired. It becomes testing time for your patience since your pursuit of practice needs repetitiveness of your meditative sessions of the mind. This may sound easy but it's rigorous in fact for certainty of results. The 'brain memory' which has been referred to earlier could be easily developed through repetitive practice of mind over and again. That is where we start losing patience and our regularity is broken. Practicing of your body and mind must be of that level that there is functional consonance between the two. We take notice of number of things in our day to day life but we do not do anything constructive knowingly or unknowingly. This is because of communication gap between 'noticing' and 'doing'. This communication gap is minimized with the help of 'brain memory' which is stored following practicing sessions of your mind. You want to be successful person in your life. That's sure. Practicing in you is essential. Doing is important. You take notice of a thing and put it into action immediately thereafter. Results are waiting there for you. Keep wining situations would become your habit ultimately.

"The 'brain memory' could be easily developed through repetitive practice of mind over and again. That is where we start losing patience and our regularity is broken. Practicing of your body and mind must be of that level that there is functional consonance between the two."

www.ingramcontent.com/pod-product-compliance
Lightning Source LLC
Chambersburg PA
CBHW030429290526
45786CB00001B/199